For FRIENDS & FAMILY

Nicky Stubbs

For FRIENDS & FAMILY

Nicky Stubbs

Human & Rousseau

First published in 2016 by Human & Rousseau,
an imprint of NB Publishers,
a division of Media24 Boeke (Pty) Ltd,
40 Heerengracht, Cape Town 8001

Commissioning editor: Annake Müller
Editor: Joy Clack, Bushbaby Editorial Services
Cover photograph and other photographs: Myburgh du Plessis, Pippa Hetherington and Diana Stubbs
Food preparation: Tani Kirsten
Food styling: Caro Alberts
Endpapers: Painting by Roy Petley. Used with permission
Book and cover design: Marius Roux, mrdesign

Reproduction by Resolution Colour (Pty) Ltd, Cape Town
Printed and bound in Malaysia by Times Offset

ISBN: 978-0-7981-7125-0

CONTENTS

10 Introduction
12 Kitchen Equipment
13 Conversions
14 Pantry Essentials

16 BREAKFAST

18 Granola
20 Stewed Fruit
22 Breakfast Porridges
~ Oats
~ Yellow Mealie Meal
~ White Mealie Meal
~ Sorghum Porridge (Maltabella)
24 French Toast
26 Omelette
28 Kedgeree
~ Kedgeree (Rich)
~ Kedgeree (Classic)
30 Sweetcorn Fritters
32 Pancakes
34 Waffles
36 Scones
38 30-day Bran Muffins

40 STARTERS, SIMPLE MEALS, VEGETABLES & SALADS

43 Starters
44 Bruschetta DIY
46 Basic Vegetable Soup
48 Onion Soup
50 Gazpacho

53 Simple Meals
54 Tomato & Pesto Quiche
56 Hamburgers & Chips
58 Pizza
60 Macaroni Cheese
62 Tuna Fishcakes
64 Bulgur Wheat Salad
66 Butternut & Coriander Couscous
68 Ratatouille
70 Lentil & Vegetable Curry
74 Bacon & Mushroom Risotto
76 Pressed Picnic Loaves

79 Vegetables
80 Lemony Mustard Green Beans
82 Melanzane
84 Baked Stuffed Peppers
86 Grilled Mixed Peppers
88 Roast Potatoes
90 Roast Potato Wedges with Rosemary
92 Baked Jacket Potatoes
94 Potato Bake
96 Cauliflower & Broccoli Cheese
98 Baked Sweet Potato & Pumpkin with Cinnamon, Brown Sugar & Orange

101 Salads
102 Green Salad & Dressing
104 Beetroot & Feta Salad
106 Cabbage Salad
108 Potato Salad with Mayonnaise
110 Potato Salad with Vinaigrette

112 MAIN MEALS

115 Chicken
116 Coq Au Vin
118 Slow-roasted Chicken with Lemon, Olives and Garlic

120 Chicken Curry
122 Chicken Pie
124 Chutney Chicken
126 Chicken Marbella
128 Roast Chicken & Vegetables

131 Beef & Lamb
132 Oxtail
134 Roast Beef & Yorkshire Pudding
136 Fillet with Béarnaise Sauce
138 Bolognaise-style Mince for Cottage Pie & Lasagne
140 Meatballs
142 Bobotie
144 Bredie
146 Slow-cooked Lamb

149 Pork
150 Slow-cooked Pork Neck on a Bed of Apples & Onions

153 Seafood
156 Paella

159 Condiments
160 Basil Pesto
162 Hummus
164 Chicken Liver Pâté
166 Tartare Sauce
168 Basic Tomato Sauce
170 Quick & Easy Mayonnaise

172 BAKING & PUDDINGS

175 Baking
176 Farm Bread
178 Lindsay's Quick & Easy Seed Loaf
180 Banana Bread
182 Buttermilk Rusks
186 Gogo van der Riet's Christmas Cake
188 Diana's Chocolate Cake
190 Chocolate Cake Using Milk Chocolate
192 Carrot Cake
194 Angel Cake
196 Lemon Polenta Cake
198 Orange Syrup Cake

200 Mum's Basic Vanilla Sponge Cake
202 Favourite Cupcakes
204 Apple Crumble
206 Baked Cheesecake
208 Chocolate Tart
210 Shortcrust Pastry
212 Lemon Meringue Pie
214 Milk Tart
216 Chocolate Roulade
218 Swiss Roll
220 Ginger Biscuits
222 Chocolate Brownies
224 Chocolate Crunchies
226 Fudge
228 Rocky Road
230 Date Squares
232 Meringues
234 Iced Profiteroles
236 Christa's Health Squares
238 Lemon Curd Squares
240 Shortbread
242 Cheese Biscuits
244 Cheese Tartlets
246 Squidgies

249 **Puddings**
250 Pears in Red Wine
252 Crème Brûlée
254 Chocolate Self-saucing Pudding
256 Malva Pudding
258 Baked Almond & Lemon Pudding
262 Traditional Christmas Pudding
264 Pavlova
266 Fruit Salad
268 Mango & Yoghurt Dessert
270 Chocolate Mousse
272 Easy Ice Cream
273 Vanilla Pod Ice Cream
274 Quick and Easy Christmas Ice Cream Bombe
276 Three Chocolate Sauces
~ Pantry Chocolate Sauce
~ Dark Chocolate Sauce
~ Bar One Chocolate Sauce
278 Custard

280 Index
285 Acknowledgements
286 About the author

Meanwhile, I have discovered no panacea for the troubles which afflict humanity – unless it is that a meal shared round the kitchen table serves both as a celebration of the good times and a comfort in times of trouble. At the end of it all, I can only echo the words of that wise old clergyman, the Reverend Sydney Smith (now there was a man for good advice): 'Take a short view of life. Look no further than dinner or tea.'

ELISABETH LUARD, *Family Life*

INTRODUCTION

As I was given a good life in a lovable world among remarkable people, mere politeness requires that I should leave a note of thanks behind. There must be a grateful record. The man who has known joy and keeps it to himself is a miser.

GUY BUTLER

This book is a love song to the family and friends who have fed me, taught me to cook, eaten and cooked with me. As I write this, I am sitting at the oval oak dining room table we ate around as a family when I was a child. It is covered in the faded grey, white and red folksy patterned tablecloth my mother used to cover a low table made of an old door and bricks for our toddler birthday parties. On the stove I am making chicken stock with the bones of a chicken I roasted to put into a pie for our Sunday lunch.

The community of cooking and food has always been central to who I am. I grew up in a home where the kitchen and dining room, simple family meals and elaborate celebrations and anniversaries revolved around cooking, eating, feeding and sharing. Meals were a cause for joy and community. My mother almost always lit candles and dimmed the lights to make every dinner an occasion, even if it was only toasted cheese before we headed out to the theatre.

Surrounded by good home cooks and cooking, I associate food with nourishment, comfort and love. I clearly remember sitting on the back step of our farmhouse as a three-year-old girl, licking out the mixing bowl my mother had used for a lemon sponge cake she had just put in the oven. Baking *her* sponge cake, generously iced with a thick butter icing, evokes a vivid recollection of her. Or my paternal grandmother's excellent tomato dish with which she extended meals when family and friends arrived unannounced. I long for my uncle's coq au vin, my maternal grandmother's apple crumble with farm cream or stewed plums that were

LEFT:
Mum holding me at Tigervlei, our farm outside Kokstad, where my heart is the happiest.

OPPOSITE:
Fishing at my Godfather, Mike le Sueur's farm in Nottingham Road.

picked off the tree that morning. I have continued the tradition of making endless batches of fudge at Christmas to give to cousins from near and far, simply because Christmas isn't as rich without the dreamy smell of butter and sugar browning on the stove.

The easy pattern with which my mother ran her kitchen was based on three meals a day, with cake and scones for high days and holidays. My father cured hams and bacon, made sausages and always made sure, whether on a farm or a smallholding outside the city, that we had a cow or two to supply us with milk and butter. Some of my most cherished memories are of visiting our grandparents, retired farmers, who lived outside Kokstad at the foot of Mount Curry in East Griqualand. A three-course breakfast was served with intent; the children were often sent into the enormous vegetable garden before lunch or supper to pick sun-warmed strawberries, beans, peas or carrots. To this day I love the sound of a carving knife being sharpened. It signals the delicious roast beef and Yorkshire pudding about to be served. My grandmother kept homemade biscuits in the blue-and-white striped Cornishware jar on the dresser next to the flask of iced water and cordial. I loved the sound of my grandmother talking quietly to her loyal and brilliant cook, Angelina, who did all of her cooking on an Aga, and the reassuring ritual of my grandfather getting up in the early morning dark in his dressing gown, to make us sandwiches for the long trip home to Johannesburg. How much better can a sandwich be than leftover mutton on farm bread?

How could I avoid falling in love with food, feeding people and eating? Recreating these dishes that have been handed down to me makes me miss these wonderful people less. And, sometimes, more.

KITCHEN EQUIPMENT

The easiest way to enjoy cooking in your kitchen is to have the right equipment. Be selective and choose the expensive appliances, knives, pots and pans carefully, as you want them to last forever. The list below includes the equipment I can't do without. I tend to shy away from gadgets as they clutter the kitchen and often create more washing up than is necessary. Also, almost inevitably, their specialised job can be as easily done using a wire whisk, a good sharp knife and a clean dishcloth.

ESSENTIALS

Stove and oven – I use an electric oven with a gas stovetop
Mixer – I chose mine based on industrial strength rather than designer looks, one of the best decisions I have made
Food processor or handheld blender
Stovetop espresso pot and metal coffee plunger
Wire whisks of different sizes
Spatulas of different sizes
A good chef's knife
A good bread knife
A collection of smaller serrated and non-serrated vegetable and paring knives
Ice-cream scoop
Nonstick lifter and metal lifter
A couple of frying pans
Good quality heavy-bottomed saucepans (at least three, in varying sizes)
Roasting pan
Baking trays (small, medium and large)
Muffin and/or shallow cupcake pans
Cake cooling rack
Cake baking tins (small, large and a ring tin is very useful)
Small pancake/omelette frying pans (it's useful to have two)
Good sturdy grater
Palette knife (invaluable for icing cakes or working with pastry)
Rolling pin
Scale
Measuring jugs and cups
Measuring spoons
A pair of scissors
Tin opener
Lemon zester
2 wooden chopping boards (at least)
1 vegetable peeler
Pastry brush
Handheld lemon squeezer or glass lemon juicer
1 handheld electric beater (not necessary if you have a large beater/mixer)
2 large metal serving spoons (useful for folding in egg whites, making meringues and having in the kitchen)
Standard loaf tin (2 for making bread)
Colander
Glass or ceramic mixing bowls (small, medium and large)
Ovenproof dishes in varying sizes
2 cooling racks
Salad bowl

Nice-to-haves

Yoghurt machine
Citrus squeezer
Ice-cream machine (both ice creams in this book can be made without a machine)
Electric citrus squeezer
Sandwich toaster (I prefer one that toasts the sandwich flat and evenly and doesn't have corrugations)

CONVERSIONS

Metric US cups

Metric	US cups
5 ml	1 tsp
15 ml	1 Tbsp
60 ml	4 Tbsp or ¼ cup
80 ml	⅓ cup
125 ml	½ cup
160 ml	⅔ cup
190 ml	¾ cup
250 ml	1 cup

Weight of 250 ml (1 cup)

Ingredient	Weight
Apricot jam	330 g
Biscuit crumbs	120 g
Breadcrumbs (dry)	60 g
Breadcrumbs (fresh)	120 g
Butter	250 g
Carrots (grated)	125 g
Cheese, grated (Gouda, Cheddar)	100 g
Cheese, grated (mozzarella)	125 g
Chocolate chips	200 g
Cocoa powder	100 g
Coconut (desiccated)	80 g
Cornflour	120 g
Cottage or cream cheese	250 g
Dates, fruitcake mix	150 g
Dried fruit	150 g
Flour (cake, self-raising, brown bread, white bread)	140 g
Honey or syrup	250 g
Nuts (chopped)	150 g
Nuts (ground almonds)	100 g
Nuts (whole)	100 g
Oats	80 g
Potatoes (grated raw)	125 g
Pumpkin (cooked, mashed)	250 g
Raisins or sultanas	150 g
Rice (uncooked)	200 g
Sugar (castor)	210 g
Sugar (icing)	130 g
Sugar (white, brown)	200 g

PANTRY ESSENTIALS

There are ingredients that I just can't do without and so I make sure that I always have sufficient to see me through to my next shop. Top of that list is good quality tinned tomatoes. My favourite are the Woolworths tinned tomatoes, which are well priced, have wonderful flavour and are not too acidic. In vague order as I arrange them in my pantry:

White cake flour
Wholewheat cake flour (small packet)
Brown bread flour
White bread flour
Self-raising flour (small packet)
Brown sugar
White sugar
Treacle sugar (small packet)
Castor sugar
Icing sugar
Cocoa powder
Bicarbonate of soda
Baking powder
Custard powder
Jelly packets (emergency pud)
Vanilla essence
Almond essence
Condensed milk
Caramel treat
Apricot jam
Tinned crushed pineapple
Tennis biscuits
Ina Paarman box cakes: vanilla and chocolate (emergency cake and brilliant for cupcakes)
Ina Paarman choc chip muffin mix
Golden Cloud crumpet and waffle mix
Tinned tomatoes
Mrs Ball's chutney
Tomato sauce (All Gold)
Extra virgin olive oil
Canola oil
Nonstick cooking spray
Red wine vinegar
White grape vinegar
Apple cider vinegar
Balsamic reduction
Brown onion soup packets
Assorted pasta
Chickpeas (dried)
Sunflower seeds
Brown rice
White rice
Risotto rice
Woolworths Salsa Nachos Chips (delicious with cream cheese if friends pop in for a drink)
Powdered vegetable, beef and chicken stock
Salt – table salt and salt flakes, such as Maldon
Black pepper
White pepper
Ground cinnamon
Ground mixed spice
Ground cumin
Ground coriander
Nutmeg
Cloves
Bay leaves
Curry powder
Dried mixed herbs

Butter wrappers – I make reference to butter wrappers or papers in some of the recipes. I use only butter in the kitchen and keep the wrappers/papers folded up in the door of the fridge. I find these useful to grease baking tins, rub hot loaves of bread, to cover roasts, and so on. It saves on baking paper and has the advantage of adding a lovely buttery flavour to any dish. If butter paper is not available or not suitable, I tear off a generous piece of greaseproof paper, run it under a tap, scrunch it up, shake it out and use that instead.

Eggs – I use extra-large eggs for all recipes and, where possible, grain-fed. They give a better colour and flavour.

Chicken stock – In most instances I default to good-quality powdered chicken stock. Current food prices make homemade chicken stock using whole fresh chickens an extravagance. I do, however, freeze all roast chicken bones, skin, carrot and spring onion peelings together in little packets until I have sufficient to make a cheat's stock. This is the stock that I use for risotto or delicate soups where the flavour of the stock is pronounced. **To make:** Place all the bones and vegetable peelings in a large lidded saucepan. Add a bay leaf, an onion roughly chopped, a carrot roughly chopped, a couple of cloves and a teaspoon of any available dried or fresh herbs. Cover with cold water and bring to the boil. Allow to simmer, with the lid half off, for about 45 minutes to an hour until the liquid has reduced to half and become flavourful. Strain and season to taste with salt and white pepper. Use immediately or freeze to store.

Mustard – There are many mustards available but I always make sure that I have the following three in stock: Pommery Moutarde de Meux, Colman's English Mustard Powder, and Colman's English Mustard.

BREAKFAST

GRANOLA

Makes 3 litres or 3 medium Ziploc® plastic bags

5 x 250 ml (5 cups) rolled oats
250 ml (1 cup) wheat germ
250 ml (1 cup) honey
190 ml (¾ cup) oil (canola or sunflower)
60 ml (¼ cup) pumpkin seeds
60 ml (¼ cup) sesame seeds
125 ml (½ cup) sunflower seeds
125 ml (½ cup) raw almonds
(or other nuts you may enjoy), chopped

1. Preheat the oven to 180 °C.
2. Place the oats and wheat germ in a bowl.
3. Stir the honey and oil together in a small saucepan over low heat until melted.
4. Add the honey mixture to the oats and wheat germ and mix.
5. Divide the granola between two baking trays and spread evenly. Bake for 15 minutes. Add the pumpkin seeds, sesame seeds, sunflower seeds and almonds, toss and bake for another 15 minutes.
6. Store in an airtight container. Can be frozen for up to four weeks.

Tip: I divide the mixture into three medium Ziploc® plastic bags, freeze two and keep only one out so that the granola stays fresh.

STEWED FRUIT

Served with Greek yoghurt and a handful of nuts, this makes a delicious start to the day.

Serves 10

1 cinnamon stick
6 whole cloves
1 litre (4 cups) water
250 ml (1 cup) sugar
a piece of orange rind shaved off using a vegetable peeler
a piece of lemon rind shaved off using a vegetable peeler
500 g mixed dried fruit

1. Place all the ingredients, except the dried fruit, in a medium-sized saucepan. Bring to the boil, allowing the sugar to dissolve.
2. Add the dried fruit, turn down the heat and simmer for 20 minutes. Allow to cool in the saucepan.
3. Serve hot or cold.

BREAKFAST PORRIDGES

Serves 4–6

OATS (add 1 handful of raisins during the cooking process; they plump up beautifully and add a touch of sweetness)

625 ml (2½ cups) water
pinch of salt
250 ml (1 cup) oats

YELLOW MEALIE MEAL (my favourite, usually available from farmstalls; at a stretch polenta can be used, but it is usually a little too fine)

1 litre (4 cups) water
pinch of salt
250 ml (1 cup) mealie meal

WHITE MEALIE MEAL

1,25 litres (5 cups) water
pinch of salt
250 ml (1 cup) mealie meal

SORGHUM PORRIDGE (Maltabella)

750 ml (3 cups) water
pinch of salt
250 ml (1 cup) Maltabella

1. Bring the water to the boil on the stove, then add the salt.
2. Pour in the grain (oats, mealie meal or sorghum) and stir with a wire whisk.
3. Bring back to the boil and then turn down the heat and simmer very gently until cooked through. Stir with the whisk from time to time.

TIP: When making all these porridges, use a wire whisk throughout cooking to prevent lumps forming.

FRENCH TOAST

French toast evolved from the necessity of using up stale baguettes. The principle remains the same today: the staler the bread, the more successfully the egg mixture will be absorbed and the crispier the toast will be. Served with bacon or even berries and cream cheese, this is a real breakfast or anytime treat.

Serves 4

190 ml (¾ cup) milk
4 extra-large eggs
pinch of salt
butter for frying (a couple of tablespoons)
8–10 slices of day-old baguette, brioche or raisin loaf
cinnamon and sugar for sprinkling
paper kitchen towel on a cake rack to absorb butter drippings

1. In a small bowl, beat the milk, eggs and salt together using a fork.
2. Pour the egg mixture into a flattish plate with raised sides (an enamel camping plate is ideal).
3. Heat half the butter in a nonstick frying pan.
4. Push the bread, a slice at a time, into the egg mixture, turning it over once and making sure that the whole slice has soaked up the milk and eggs.
5. Transfer immediately into the hot butter and fry on both sides until golden brown. Only fry three to four slices at a time.
6. Once cooked, move onto the kitchen towel to pat off the surplus butter, sprinkle with cinnamon and sugar and serve immediately.

OMELETTE

As to the omelette itself, it seems to me to be a confection which demands the most straightforward approach. What one wants is the taste of the fresh eggs and the fresh butter and, visually, a soft bright golden roll plump and spilling out a little at the edges. It should not be a busy, important urban dish but something gentle and pastoral, with the clean scent of the dairy, the kitchen garden, the basket of early morning mushrooms or the sharp tang of freshly picked herbs, sorrel, chives, tarragon. And although there are those who maintain that wine and egg dishes don't go together I must say I do regard a glass or two of wine as not, obviously, essential but at least as an enormous enhancement of the enjoyment of a well-cooked omelette.

But we are not in any case considering the great occasion menu but the almost primitive and elemental meal evoked by the words: Let's just have an omelette and a glass of wine.

Elizabeth David

Serves 1

3 extra-large eggs (per omelette)
pinch of salt
pinch of white pepper
15 ml (1 Tbsp) butter

1. In a small bowl, beat the eggs, salt and pepper together with a fork.
2. Melt the butter in the frying pan until just sizzling but not browning.
3. Pour the egg mixture gently into the pan, allowing it to cover the base.
4. The omelette will cook through from the bottom. Keep an eye on the mixture as it should not cook through entirely – there should still be a trail of uncooked egg. Once almost all the liquid egg has cooked and firmed, gently roll up the omelette and slide it onto a warmed plate.
5. Serve immediately.

Tips:

~ Key to the success of a good omelette is a flat-bottomed, good quality pan. Any scratches will make the egg stick and frustrate your efforts and good intentions.
~ If you enjoy an omelette that is not quite as simple, add grated cheese, chopped ham or diced fried bacon, sautéed onions and mushrooms or just about anything you enjoy, at the last stage before rolling up and serving.

KEDGEREE

Even though it is traditionally served for breakfast or brunch, my maternal grandmother often made kedgeree for supper. Although it has fallen out of fashion, this simple dish is nourishing, satisfying and ridiculously easy to make. Western kedgeree consists of flaked fish, boiled eggs and rice. In India, where the dish originated, *khichari* refers to many different grain and legume dishes.

Kedgeree (Rich)

Serves 6

180 g basmati rice
500 g smoked haddock fillets, defrosted
500 ml (2 cups) milk
lemon rind, large thumb-size piece
2 bay leaves
30 ml (2 Tbsp) butter
30 ml (2 Tbsp) cake flour
15 ml (1 Tbsp) Dijon mustard
1 bunch spring onions, finely chopped (optional)
salt and black pepper
1 handful of chopped fresh parsley, to serve
3 hard-boiled extra-large eggs, chopped (optional)

1. Preheat the oven to 180 °C.
2. Cook the rice in boiling salted water, then drain and set aside.
3. Place the haddock in a small ovenproof dish with the milk, lemon rind and bay leaves. Bake for 20 minutes until cooked through. Remove from the milk and flake into large chunks. Reserve the milk.
4. Melt the butter in a saucepan. Whisk in the flour, followed by the reserved milk, stirring all the time. When the mixture starts to thicken, stir in the mustard and spring onions, and season with salt and pepper. Just before the mixture boils, remove from the heat.
5. Mix the fish and rice gently into the sauce. Place in a warmed serving dish and sprinkle with parsley and chopped eggs.

Variation: Kedgeree (Classic)

If kedgeree without the white sauce is preferred, cook the fish in half milk, half water. Mix the rice and cooked, flaked fish together with a fork and toss in a tablespoon of butter to melt through. Place in a warmed serving dish and sprinkle with parsley and chopped eggs.

SWEETCORN FRITTERS

I dream of sitting down to a breakfast prepared by my mother that includes her sweetcorn fritters nestled between home-cured bacon and fried eggs. Served on holidays or birthdays, these delicious fritters elevated breakfast to a celebration.

Makes 6–8

1 tin (410 g) whole kernel sweetcorn, drained
375 ml (1½ cups) cake flour
2 extra-large eggs
125 ml (½ cup) milk
5 ml (1 tsp) baking powder
pinch of salt
canola oil for frying
paper kitchen towel, for draining

1. Mix all the ingredients, except the oil, in a bowl using a fork or wire whisk.
2. Heat the oil – enough to cover the base of the frying pan – until a teaspoon of mixture dropped in sizzles.
3. Drop tablespoonfuls of the mixture into the hot (but not smoking) oil.
4. Fry gently for 3–4 minutes per side until golden brown.
5. Drain on kitchen towel and serve. If not serving immediately, keep the fritters warm in a warming drawer or in an oven on low heat.

PANCAKES

Makes 16–18

500 ml (2 cups) cake flour
2,5 ml (½ tsp) baking powder
pinch of salt
325 ml (1⅓ cups) milk
325 ml (1⅓ cups) water
2 extra-large eggs
15 ml (1 Tbsp) canola oil
butter for frying
cinnamon sugar, to serve

1. Mix all the ingredients, except the butter and cinnamon sugar, in a bowl or jug using a wire whisk. Using a jug makes pouring the mixture into the pan much easier. Allow the mixture to stand for at least 30 minutes. This allows for a lighter pancake.
2. Heat a knob of butter in a pancake or omelette pan (no scratches or the pancake mixture will stick). When the butter has melted, take a piece of kitchen towel and wipe off any excess butter. Keep the buttery kitchen paper to give the pan a wipe in between pancakes.
3. Pour just enough pancake batter into the frying pan, tilting the pan to ensure the base is covered. It should not be thickly covered; the thinner the better.
4. Allow to cook through on one side until little bubbles form in the mixture and the sides become feathery and lacy. Turn the pancake with a spatula and cook the other side.
5. Remove to a warmed plate and sprinkle with cinnamon sugar. If not serving immediately, keep warm on a warmed plate covered with a slightly damp dishcloth.

WAFFLES

Makes 8 medium waffles

2 extra-large eggs
500 ml (2 cups) cake flour
450 ml (1¾ cups) milk
125 ml (½ cup) canola oil
15 ml (1 Tbsp) sugar
20 ml (4 tsp) baking powder
1 ml (¼ tsp) salt
2,5 ml (½ tsp) vanilla essence

1. Heat the waffle machine. Spray generously with nonstick cooking spray.
2. Using a wire whisk, mix all the ingredients in a bowl until smooth.
3. Pour the waffle batter onto the hot waffle plate, about 125 ml (½ cup) of mixture at a time. Remove once cooked through and golden brown. Spray the machine waffle surface when necessary.
4. Serve hot or at room temperature.

SCONES

Makes 8–10

There is nothing worse than a badly made scone, especially those made in a microwave oven. Scones, baked properly, are the ultimate teatime treat. My mother's scones were always served with homemade apricot or strawberry jam with thick farm cream and butter. Mum would magic them up out of nowhere if friends popped in or at teatime after a long Sunday lunch.

500 ml (2 cups) cake flour
15 ml (1 Tbsp) baking powder
pinch of salt
30 ml (2 Tbsp) sugar
125 g butter
1 extra-large egg
100 ml plain yoghurt, amasi or buttermilk
45 ml (3 Tbsp) water

1. Preheat the oven to 200 °C. Grease a baking tray with butter or nonstick cooking spray.
2. Sift the dry ingredients together.
3. Cut and rub in the butter until the mixture resembles breadcrumbs.
4. In a small bowl, beat the egg, yoghurt and water together with a fork.
5. Add the liquid to the dry ingredients and, using your fingers, bring the mixture together very lightly.
6. Turn out onto a floured surface, shape gently and pat down slightly. Cut out the scones using a floured cookie cutter or a floured sharp knife.
7. Bake for 15 minutes until just starting to turn golden.
8. Cool on a cake rack and serve as fresh as possible.

30-DAY BRAN MUFFINS

Makes 20 small muffins

2 extra-large eggs
125 ml (½ cup) canola oil
250 g brown sugar
10 ml (2 tsp) vanilla essence
500 ml (2 cups) digestive bran
300 g cake flour
10 ml (2 tsp) bicarbonate of soda
125 ml (½ cup) raisins, currants, dates or a combination of the three
500 ml (2 cups) milk or buttermilk

1. Using a wire whisk, mix all the ingredients together in a bowl. If you are going to store the mixture in the fridge and make the muffins as you need them, use a bowl with a lid or cover with plastic wrap. The theory is that this mixture lasts for 30 days in the fridge. We have never had the opportunity to test that theory as they are eaten far too quickly!
2. Preheat the oven to 180 °C. Spray a muffin pan or a cupcake pan with nonstick cooking spray. I prefer using the shallow old-fashioned cupcake pans so that the muffins are not too big. If the muffins are being made to pack into school lunchboxes or to be transported, use small baking cups.
3. Spoon the mixture into the pans or baking cups to three-quarters full.
4. Bake for 15–20 minutes until firm and springy to the touch.
5. Serve hot or at room temperature. They can be frozen for six weeks.

Tip: Chopped nuts can be added or a combination of cinnamon and brown sugar sprinkled on top just before they go into the oven.

STARTERS, SIMPLE MEALS, VEGETABLES & SALADS

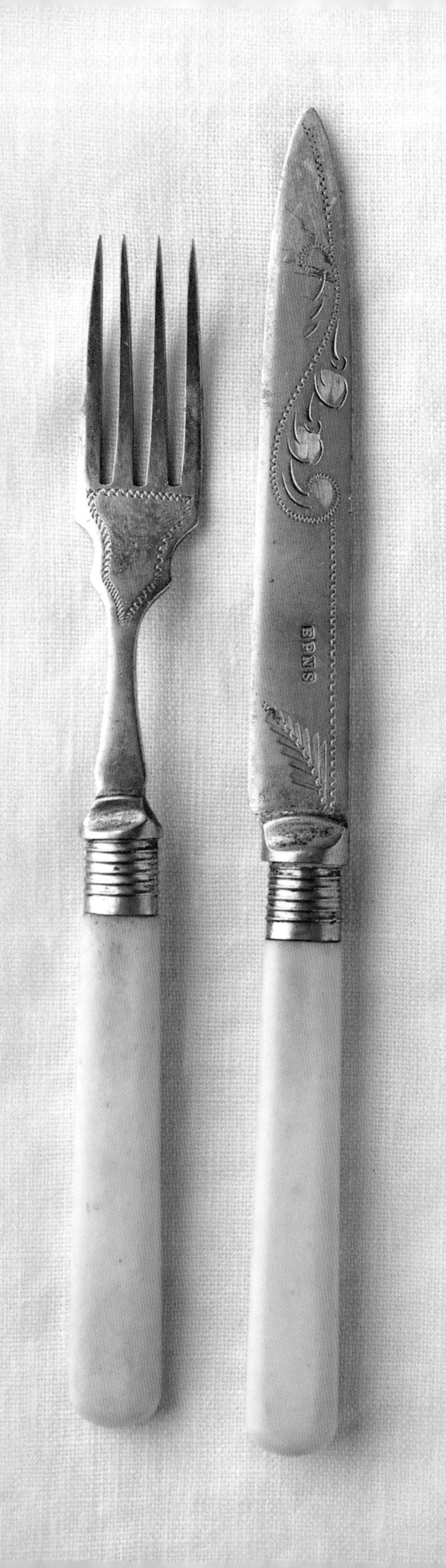
EPNS

STARTERS

BRUSCHETTA DIY

(served as an antipasto on the table)

Serves 4–6

white farm-style or ciabatta bread, thickly sliced and grilled or toasted both sides (at least 2 slices each)
6 or more cloves garlic, peeled and left whole and served in a small bowl
olive oil served in a small bowl with a teaspoon or in a spouted bottle, or simply in its own bottle
balsamic vinegar served in a small bowl with a teaspoon or in a spouted bottle, or simply in its own bottle
6 or more ripe flavourful tomatoes (Italian or rosa), thickly sliced
1 handful of fresh basil, roughly torn and served in a little bowl
sea salt and black pepper

Serve all the ingredients attractively laid out on the table top and encourage guests to help themselves. Rub the garlic straight onto one side of the bread, drizzle with olive oil (and vinegar if liked) and then top with tomato and basil. Sprinkle on the salt and grind over pepper.

VARIATIONS:

Chopped olives; capers; anchovies; Basil Pesto (see page 160); tapenade and so on.

BASIC VEGETABLE SOUP

Serves 6

30 ml (2 Tbsp) butter
1 onion, chopped
2 stalks celery, chopped (optional)
4 *x* 250 ml (4 cups) chopped vegetables (pumpkin, carrot, butternut, courgette [baby marrow], potato, peas, sweet potato, broccoli), using either a single vegetable or a combination of choice
45 ml (3 Tbsp) cake flour
pinch of curry powder (optional)
pinch of nutmeg
5 ml (1 tsp) dried mixed herbs
1,25 litres (5 cups) chicken stock
salt and white pepper
chopped fresh parsley, for garnishing

1. Melt the butter in a large saucepan and add the onion and celery. Fry gently until soft but not brown.
2. Add the vegetables and fry gently for 2–3 minutes.
3. Mix in the flour, curry powder, nutmeg and mixed herbs.
4. Pour in the chicken stock, bring to a slow boil, turn down the heat, and simmer for 20 minutes until the vegetables are cooked through.
5. Blend the soup with a handheld blender.
6. Serve hot or cold, garnished with chopped parsley.
7. Store in the fridge. It can be frozen for 3–4 weeks.

ONION SOUP

When I was 14, our father – then in his forties – took our family on a whirlwind tour of Europe: *Europe on 20 dollars a day*. It was his first time overseas. One of my most precious memories from that trip was Dad's determination to find a particular onion soup from a particular bistro tucked away in a side street. The wonders of Paris were eclipsed for me by the onion soup experience as the longest diary entry for the whole tour was 'We had delicious onion soup for lunch and it was delicious'. Our father taught us to always seek out the finest and do our best, even if it was only finding the best onion soup.

Serves 8

1 kg brown onions, thinly sliced
60 g butter
15 ml (1 Tbsp) canola or olive oil
salt and white pepper
pinch of brown sugar
2 litres (8 cups) hot beef stock (use liquid stock sachets rather than powdered stock)
splash of white vermouth or dry sherry to taste (optional)
sliced baguettes (2 per serving), toasted
150 g Gruyère (or other strongly flavoured) cheese, grated

1. In a large saucepan, cook the onions very slowly in the butter and oil, with the lid on, for 15 minutes. Do not allow to brown.
2. Remove the lid, add the salt and sugar, turn up the heat slightly and cook for 30 minutes until the onions are a deep golden brown. Do not allow to burn, and stir from time to time.
3. Remove from the heat and add the hot stock and vermouth or sherry if using. Season to taste.
4. Leave to simmer, partially covered, for another 45 minutes. Season to taste.
5. When serving, place the toast in the warmed soup bowls, sprinkle over the cheese and pour the soup over the bread and cheese. This will melt the cheese slightly and the bread will float to the top.
6. Serve piping hot.

Tip: The trick to onion soup, with its simple and humble ingredients, is time and a good stock. The longer this soup cooks, the better the flavour.

GAZPACHO

Serves 6–8

Our wedding was held at a nineteenth-century Anglican mission church in Ladybrand in the Free State. Long tables with white tablecloths were set up in the old sandstone house. The centrepiece of each table was a soup tureen filled with delicious, refreshing gazpacho. Simple, grand and perfect.

2 tins (410 g each) chopped Italian tomatoes, chilled
1 small red or yellow pepper, finely diced
1 cucumber, peeled and sliced
1 onion, quartered
3 stalks celery, chopped
15 ml (1 Tbsp) finely chopped fresh parsley
1 small clove garlic
1 litre (4 cups) chicken stock, chilled
15 ml (1 Tbsp) red wine vinegar or apple cider vinegar
45–60 ml (3–4 Tbsp) extra virgin olive oil
2 small tins (200 ml each) tomato cocktail, chilled
10 ml (2 tsp) Worcestershire sauce
salt and pepper, to taste

1. Blend all the ingredients together in batches. Do not blend very smooth as gazpacho is better with a bit of texture and crunch.
2. Chill for at least 4 hours.
3. Serve in chilled soup bowls or glasses with cheese straws, focaccia or other simple, hearty bread on the side.

SIMPLE MEALS

TOMATO & PESTO QUICHE

Serves 4

1 quantity Shortcrust Pastry (see page 210) made with 100 g butter

FILLING

handful of rosa tomatoes, washed
handful of basil leaves
30 ml (2 Tbsp) Basil Pesto (see page 160)
100 g Parmesan cheese, grated
3 extra-large eggs
250 ml (1 cup) fresh cream

1. Preheat the oven to 190 °C.
2. Line a 23-cm quiche dish with the pastry and prick the bottom with a fork.
3. Bake in the oven for 10 minutes to partially cook the pastry (it shouldn't brown).
4. Remove the pastry shell from the oven. Arrange the tomatoes in the pastry shell. Scatter over the basil leaves.
5. Mix the remaining filling ingredients together and pour over the tomatoes and basil to fill the pastry case.
6. Bake for 35–40 minutes until slightly browned on top and set.
7. Serve hot or at room temperature.

HAMBURGERS & CHIPS

Makes 10 burger patties

1 kg lean mince (beef or a mixture of beef, pork and lamb)
1 onion, chopped
1 extra-large egg
2 carrots, grated
2,5 ml (½ tsp) ground cinnamon (optional)
5 ml (1 tsp) dried mixed herbs
salt and pepper
15 ml (1 Tbsp) Dijon mustard or 1–2 gherkins, finely chopped

OVEN CHIPS

1 potato per person, sliced lengthwise into eighths with the skin still on
extra virgin olive oil or canola oil
salt and pepper
dried mixed herbs

1. Using your hands, mix all the burger ingredients together very well.
2. Shape into 10 balls and flatten slightly.
3. Heat olive oil or sunflower oil in a frying pan and fry for 10 minutes in total, turning now and then.
4. To make the chips, preheat the oven to 200 °C.
5. Place the cut potatoes onto two large baking trays. Rub with oil, salt and pepper and herbs.
6. Bake for 45 minutes – do not turn – or until golden brown and crisp.
7. Assemble the burgers as you prefer and serve with the chips.

PIZZA

Makes 1 exra-large or 2 large pizzas

DOUGH

600 g bread or cake flour, plus extra for rolling
pinch of salt
10 g active yeast
400 ml lukewarm water
30 ml (2 Tbsp) tomato paste (a tube is useful and easy to use)

TOPPINGS

mozzarella or cheese of your choice, grated
Suggestions for additional toppings: sliced onions, crushed garlic, olives, sliced mushrooms, sliced peppers, capers, sun-dried tomatoes, artichokes in olive oil, ham, salami, feta, fresh or dried herbs etc. Add avocado, rocket and other fresh ingredients once the pizza is cooked.

1. Mix the flour, salt and yeast together in a bowl. Make a well in the mixture.
2. Add the water and mix with your hands to form a smooth dough.
3. Sprinkle flour over the work surface and knead the dough very well.
4. Set the dough aside in a clean bowl, covered by a damp cloth or plastic wrap, in a warm place for at least 30 minutes. The dough will double in size.
5. Preheat the oven to its highest setting, around 230 °C, and put a baking tray into the oven.
6. Roll out the dough and spread the tomato paste over it.
7. Take the baking tray out of the oven with oven gloves and gently lift the pizza dough onto the baking tray.
8. Sprinkle on your choice of toppings.
9. Pop into the oven and bake for about 8 minutes.
10. Eat while it is still hot.

MACARONI CHEESE

Serves 4–5

250 g pasta (macaroni)
60 g butter
60 g cake flour
600 ml (2⅖ cups) milk
300 g good Cheddar cheese, grated
salt and pepper
5 ml (1 tsp) Dijon mustard
3 tomatoes, sliced (optional)
salad, to serve

1. Preheat the oven to 180 °C. Grease a shallow ovenproof dish.
2. Boil the pasta according to the instructions on the box.
3. Melt the butter in a saucepan. Remove from the heat and add the flour, mixing it in with a wire whisk. Return to the heat.
4. Stirring all the time, add the milk. Keep stirring over medium heat until the sauce thickens. Just as it starts to boil, take the saucepan off the heat.
5. Add most of the grated cheese and stir in.
6. Season to taste with salt and pepper and the Dijon mustard.
7. Mix the sauce and cooked, drained pasta together.
8. Pour half the mixture into the ovenproof dish. Layer the sliced tomato on top of the mixture. Place the remaining mixture on top of the tomato and top with grated cheese.
9. Bake for 30 minutes until the cheese on top has melted and is starting to brown.
10. Serve warm with a salad.

TUNA FISHCAKES

Makes 12 fishcakes

4 potatoes
2 tins (170 g each) tuna
¼ onion or 4 spring onions, very finely chopped
2 extra-large eggs
30 ml (2 Tbsp) Dijon mustard
chopped fresh parsley (optional)
salt and pepper
125 ml (½ cup) cake flour
15 ml (1 Tbsp) butter
30 ml (2 Tbsp) olive oil (or other oil)
paper kitchen towel, for draining

1. Peel the potatoes and boil for about 25 minutes until soft.
2. Drain the tuna.
3. Mash the tuna and potatoes together with a fork.
4. Add the onion, eggs, mustard, parsley, salt and pepper.
5. Using your hands, form the mixture into 12 balls, place on a baking tray and then flatten slightly. Cover with a wet teatowel and place in the fridge for 30 minutes.
6. Put the flour into a shallow plate. Roll each fishcake lightly in the flour.
7. Melt the butter and oil together in a frying pan.
8. Fry the fishcakes on both sides, turning once, until golden brown.
9. Place the fishcakes on paper kitchen towel to drain off the excess oil, cover and keep warm until needed. Do not keep in a warming drawer for longer than 1 hour. If you are not eating them immediately, allow to cool and keep in the fridge until required. The fishcakes can also be eaten cold or heated up in the microwave oven.

BULGUR WHEAT SALAD

Serves 6–8

375 ml (1½ cups) bulgur wheat (cracked wheat) or stampkoring
1 bunch spring onions, finely chopped
375 ml (1½ cups) chopped fresh parsley
125 ml (½ cup) chopped fresh mint
1 large ripe tomato, choppped
125 ml (½ cup) olive oil
80 ml (⅓ cup) lemon juice
salt and pepper, to taste

1. If using bulghur wheat, pour over hot water and allow to stand for 2 hours. If using stampkoring, boil in salted water for 30 minutes until chewy.
2. Combine all the ingredients in a large bowl and mix well.
3. Serve chilled.
4. This salad will keep for three to four days, covered, in the fridge.

BUTTERNUT & CORIANDER COUSCOUS

Serves 6–8

1 packet butternut pieces, cut into squares or 1 small to medium butternut, peeled and chopped
olive oil
sea salt and pepper
250 g couscous, prepared as per instructions on box
175 ml Hummus (see page 162)
10 ml (2 tsp) ground cumin
500 ml (2 cups) thick Greek yoghurt
1 tin (410 g) chickpeas, drained or 100 g dried chickpeas, soaked, cooked and drained
1 tin (410 g) brown lentils, drained or 100 g dried brown lentils, cooked and drained
1 handful of pumpkin seeds
1 generous handful of fresh coriander (dhania), to garnish

1. Preheat the oven to 180 °C.
2. Place the butternut on a roasting tray, rub generously with olive oil and salt, and season with pepper. Place in the oven and roast for 35–45 minutes until fragrant, soft and browning on the edges.
3. While the butternut is cooking, make up the couscous and set aside. Fork through to prevent lumps.
4. Mix the hummus and cumin into the yoghurt and season with salt and pepper.
5. Place the couscous on a platter, then scatter over the chickpeas, lentils and pumpkin seeds. Arrange the butternut on top.
6. Place dollops of the yoghurt dressing over the butternut and couscous, and sprinkle over the coriander.
7. Serve at room temperature.

RATATOUILLE

Serves 8 as a side dish

As a side dish with any roast, as a starter sprinkled with Parmesan, or simply eaten on its own, ratatouille is versatile and can be served hot, cold or at room temperature. Ratatouille shouldn't be a lumpy vegetable stew, but rather a carefully made layering of complementary vegetables. The wonderful Disney movie *Ratatouille* takes this wholesome, nourishing dish to new heights. It also brilliantly shows how food and eating can evoke childhood memories and call up the nostalgia of home better than anything else.

3 peppers (red, yellow and orange), cored and thickly sliced
1 large aubergine (brinjal), thickly sliced
small punnet courgettes (baby marrows), cut into chunks
125 ml (½ cup) extra virgin olive oil
salt and black pepper
2 onions (red if available), sliced
2–3 cloves garlic, chopped
2 tins (410 g each) chopped Italian tomatoes
5 ml (1 tsp) brown sugar
1 punnet fresh basil

1. Preheat the oven to 190 °C.
2. Place the peppers, aubergine and courgettes in a roomy baking dish, pour in the olive oil and season with salt and pepper. Using your hands, rub the vegetables all over to make sure they are covered in oil.
3. Roast for 20 minutes.
4. Add the onions and garlic in a layer and mix in gently. Roast for another 20 minutes.
5. Pour over the chopped tomatoes evenly, sprinkle with sugar, season with salt and pepper and return to the oven for another 20 minutes.
6. If serving hot, mix in the basil leaves and serve immediately. The heat will blacken the basil leaves. If serving at room temperature or cold, add the basil leaves just before serving, scattered on top.

Tip: Pitted black olives, capers and anchovies can be added to turn this into a more substantial dish.

LENTIL & VEGETABLE CURRY

Serves 6

3 onions
3 large cloves garlic, chopped
45 ml (3 Tbsp) canola or olive oil
2 carrots, sliced
4–6 potatoes, peeled and chopped
1 thumb-length piece of fresh ginger root, finely chopped or grated
6 whole cloves
6 cardamom pods
1 cinnamon stick
10 ml (2 tsp) chilli powder or 2–3 small chillies, seeded and chopped
5 ml (1 tsp) turmeric
15 ml (1 Tbsp) ground cumin
1 tin (410 g) tomatoes
250 ml (1 cup) dried brown lentils
750 ml (3 cups) vegetable or chicken stock
125 ml (½ cup) frozen peas, defrosted
125 ml (½ cup) fresh cream or plain yoghurt (optional)

1. Sauté the onions and garlic in the oil until flavourful and slightly browned.
2. Add the carrots, potatoes and ginger, and cook for a further 4–5 minutes.
3. Add the cloves, cardamom, cinnamon, chilli, turmeric and cumin and cook for another couple of minutes.
4. Add the tomatoes, stirring the bottom of the pan to lift any browned residue and to incorporate its colour and flavour into the liquid of the tomatoes.
5. Add the lentils and the stock and cook over medium heat for 35–45 minutes until the lentils are soft.
6. Just before serving, add the frozen peas. They do not have to cook through; they should simply be stirred into the hot curry.
7. If a richer and slightly milder curry is preferred, stir in the cream or yoghurt at the very last moment, heat through and serve.

Right: Bacon & Mushroom Risotto, recipe on page 74

BACON & MUSHROOM RISOTTO

The queen of comfort foods, risotto is straightforward and easy to make. This recipe evolved from ingredients I almost always have in my kitchen.

I freeze the chicken bones left over from roast chicken or chicken casseroles to make stock for soups or risotto. To make the stock, place the bones (frozen or not) in a saucepan, cover with cold water and bring to the boil on the stove. Turn down to a simmer and allow to reduce, lid off, until a good flavourful stock has developed. If you have time and the inclination, it can be improved by adding a couple of celery stalks or leaves, a sliced carrot and bouquet garni or bay leaf. Otherwise, I find the liquid stock concentrate in sachets, to which water is added, have a good flavour. (See chicken stock notes on page 15)

Serves 4–6

1 packet bacon, diced
30 ml (2 Tbsp) olive oil
2 cloves garlic, crushed
1 onion, finely chopped
1–1,5 litres (4–6 cups) chicken stock
500 g mixed chopped mushrooms (portabellini give the best flavour)
splash of white wine if you have a bottle open
250 g risotto (short grain) rice
15 ml (1 Tbsp) chopped fresh herbs (parsley, thyme, sage)
15 ml (1 Tbsp) butter
grated Parmesan cheese, to serve

1. In a roomy heavy-bottomed saucepan, gently fry the bacon in the olive oil until just cooked.
2. Add the garlic and onion and sweat slowly until translucent.
3. While the garlic and onion are cooking, place another saucepan on the stove and bring the stock to a low simmer.
4. Add the chopped mushrooms to the garlic and onion mixture, stir together well with a wooden spoon, place the lid on and simmer until the mushrooms have softened and become flavourful.
5. If you are using wine, add it at this stage and allow the liquid to cook off, leaving behind its characteristic flavour.
6. Add the rice and stir in well, allowing the vegetables and oil to coat each grain.
7. Gradually add the stock (I use a soup ladle), stirring well in between ladlefuls. Allow the rice to absorb the liquid before adding the next spoonful. This process takes between 15 and 20 minutes, depending on how you prefer your risotto. The rice should be creamy but not mushy.
8. Once the rice has softened and is almost cooked, remove from the heat, stir in the chopped herbs and butter, cover with the lid and leave to stand and swell for 5–10 minutes.
9. Serve with grated Parmesan cheese.

Optional extra: I sometimes add 1 handful of frozen peas (petit pois if possible) just before leaving the risotto to stand. They add a lovely colour and sweetness to the dish.

PRESSED PICNIC LOAVES

I have made these pressed sandwiches for beach picnics, mountain walks, camping trips and road trips. Country bread is traditionally used in France, but I find ciabatta extremely good as it is not too bready, absorbs olive oil well and is a convenient size and shape to press, transport and slice. The filling can be adapted to your taste, as long as it shouts summer and fun.

Serves 6

1 large ciabatta
olive oil for drizzling
1 clove garlic, peeled
Grilled Mixed Peppers (see page 86)
½ red onion, sliced or 1 bunch spring onions, sliced
torn basil leaves or Basil Pesto (see page 160)
stuffed or pitted green olives, drained
2 balls mozzarella, sliced
3 roma or other Italian tomatoes, thinly sliced
12 slices salami or other flavourful cured meat
salt and pepper
drained capers, anchovies, sliced boiled egg, chopped fresh parsley (optional)

1. Cut the ciabatta loaf in half horizontally.
2. Drizzle olive oil on both sides and rub with the garlic. Discard the used garlic.
3. Assemble the sandwich in layers as above, closing it off with the top half of the ciabatta.
4. Tightly wrap the whole sandwich in plastic wrap, making sure to press it together as tightly as possible. Store overnight or for at least 4 hours under a heavy weight in the fridge. Putting a baking tray between the sandwich and the weight helps to distribute the weight evenly.
5. Transport the sandwich in the plastic wrap. Just before serving, transfer to clean brown paper or greaseproof paper, or slice on a wooden board with a sharp knife.

OPEN

VEGETABLES

LEMONY MUSTARD GREEN BEANS

Serves 6–8 as a side dish

600 g fine green beans
50 g (½ cup) hazelnuts
125 ml (½ cup) fresh cream
10 ml (2 tsp) Dijon mustard
juice of 1 lemon
salt and pepper

1. Trim the beans and boil briefly in salted water for 5 minutes. Drain immediately in a sieve or colander and run cold water over them to halt the cooking process. Keep aside until ready to serve.
2. Preheat the oven to 200 °C.
3. Place the hazelnuts on a baking tray and place in the oven for 7–10 minutes until the skins have blackened. Remove from the oven and allow to cool. Using a teatowel, rub off the skins. Store in an airtight container until used.
4. Mix the cream, mustard and lemon juice together, and season to taste with salt and pepper. Store, covered, in the fridge until needed.
5. Drizzle the cream dressing over the beans, sprinkle with the chopped, toasted hazelnuts and serve immediately. Serve as a starter with crusty bread or as a side dish with roasts.

MELANZANE

Serves 4 as a main dish

3 medium aubergines (brinjals)
salt
2 cloves garlic, finely chopped
1 tin (410 g) tomatoes
olive oil
45 ml (3 Tbsp) Basil Pesto (see page 160)
1 handful of fresh basil leaves, roughly torn
300 g (2 cups) mozzarella cheese, cut into slices
50 g (½ cup) Parmesan cheese, grated

1. Preheat the oven to 180 °C.
2. Slice the aubergines lengthwise, sprinkle with salt and leave to sweat for about 30 minutes.
3. Place the garlic and tinned tomatoes in a saucepan, bring to the boil and simmer for 15 minutes until the tomatoes have softened and the garlic has released its flavour. Add the pesto and allow to cool.
4. Rinse the salt off the aubergines, pat dry and brush both sides with olive oil. Place on a baking tray in the oven for 30 minutes until softened.
5. Layer the tomato sauce, aubergines, basil leaves, mozzarella cheese slices and Parmesan, in that order, in an ovenproof dish, repeating the layering to use up all the ingredients. Finish off with the Parmesan cheese.
6. Bake for 30 minutes until the top is slightly browned. Serve hot or at room temperature.

BAKED STUFFED PEPPERS

½ pepper per person as a side dish
1 pepper per person as a starter or main dish

4–5 mixed peppers
1 tin (410 g) chopped Italian tomatoes
1 packet (200 g) calamata olives (preferably pitted)
200 g (2 cups) feta cheese, broken into chunks
olive oil
sea salt and pepper
fresh herbs of choice (chopped parsley always works well)

1. Preheat the oven to 180 °C. Line a baking tray with foil.
2. Slice each pepper in half (vertically) and remove the pith, seeds and stalk as far as possible, keeping the pepper shell intact.
3. Spoon the chopped tomatoes into the halved peppers. Scatter over the olives and chunks of feta cheese.
4. Drizzle olive oil over the peppers – be generous – and season with salt and pepper.
5. Bake for 30 minutes until the peppers are just starting to brown.
6. Serve hot or at room temperature, scattered with herbs. Serve as a starter or main dish for vegetarians.

GRILLED MIXED PEPPERS

Serves 6 as side dish

4 peppers, mixed colours (red, green, yellow)
190 ml (¾ cup) olive oil
salt and black pepper
chopped fresh herbs (basil, thyme, origanum or parsley, or a combination)
olives (optional)
capers (optional)
anchovies (optional)
15 ml (1 Tbsp) Basil Pesto (see page 160, optional)

1. Preheat the oven grill.
2. Place the peppers on a baking tray.
3. Roast the peppers under the grill, watching closely and turning once one side is blackened in places. Once the other side has also blackened, remove from the oven and run under cold water.
4. Remove the skins as far as possible.
5. Remove the core and pith and slice the peppers.
6. Toss in the olive oil and season to taste.
7. Serve on a plate with any of or a combination of the rest of the ingredients.

ROAST POTATOES

Much is written about the ultimate roast potato, but as with many of the classics, keep it simple and as unfussy as possible. Don't hover, and allow the starch in the potato and hot oil to do the trick. One large floury potato per diner, plus a couple extra is a good way to make sure you will have enough.

Serves 6

6–8 large floury potatoes, peeled
125 ml (½ cup) canola oil
paper kitchen towel, for draining
salt

1. Preheat the oven to 200 °C.
2. Place the potatoes in a large saucepan, cover with cold water, add a pinch of salt and bring to the boil. Allow to boil fast for 5 minutes and then turn off the heat.
3. While the potatoes are coming to the boil, pour the oil into a large, roomy baking tray (the potatoes should not fit snugly, but must have the surface area exposed to the oil) and place in the oven. If your joint or chicken is in the oven at a lower temperature, don't worry, simply cook the potatoes a little longer. The oil needs to heat up before you add the potatoes to ensure that they crisp from the start.
4. Drain the parboiled potatoes very well and dry off. Cut into egg-size pieces and scatter into the preheated oil.
5. Roast for between 45 minutes and 1 hour, depending on what else is in the oven and on the type of potato you have used. Give the pan a shake halfway through cooking and turn the potatoes so that all sides become golden brown and crisp.
6. Drain the potatoes on paper kitchen towel (I like to use a colander lined with kitchen paper to do this). Sprinkle with salt and serve immediately.

ROAST POTATO WEDGES WITH ROSEMARY

Serves 6

6 medium-sized potatoes
olive oil
sea salt and black pepper
5–6 sprigs fresh rosemary or 15 ml (1 Tbsp) dried rosemary (or thyme)

1. Preheat the oven to 190 °C.
2. Cut each potato into eighths (lengthwise like chips), leaving the skins on. Scatter loosely in a baking or roasting pan.
3. Using your hands, rub the potatoes with generous amounts of olive oil, salt and pepper. Scatter the rosemary under, over and among the potatoes, rubbing off some of the leaves to stick to the potatoes.
4. Place in the oven for 45 minutes without touching them. Don't be tempted to give them a stir, or they end up steaming and not browning sufficiently.
5. After 45 minutes, once they have started browning, turn them and cook for a further 10–15 minutes until sizzling in places and well browned.
6. Serve hot.

BAKED JACKET POTATOES

Often forgotten about, a baked potato makes a wonderfully simple and nourishing lunch. If the potato skins are rubbed with oil, they do not require pricking. The variety of potato used is important so make sure to check if the potatoes are good for baking.

1 large baking potato per person
olive oil or canola oil
salt – flaked sea salt is good but if not available, table salt works just as well
grated cheese, tuna mayonnaise or a knob of butter to serve

1. Preheat the oven to 200°C.
2. Rub each potato with oil and salt and place on a baking tray.
3. Bake for 1 hour.
4. Remove from the oven, cut each potato in half and top with cheese, tuna mayonnaise or a knob of butter.

POTATO BAKE

Serves 8–10 as a side dish

100 g butter
1 kg potatoes, sliced (I prefer to leave the skin on, but if you prefer, peel the potatoes at this stage)
salt and white pepper
375 ml (1½ cups) fresh cream
375 ml (1½ cups) milk

1. Preheat the oven to 190 °C.
2. Rub a large, flat serving dish with half of the butter.
3. Layer the potatoes in the dish, adding small knobs of the remaining butter and seasoning as you layer.
4. Warm the cream and milk through, but don't boil.
5. Pour the cream and milk mixture over the potatoes and flatten gently so that the potatoes are almost covered with the mixture.
6. Cover the potatoes with wet, wrung out baking paper (I keep and re-use butter paper; see page 15) and place in the oven.
7. Bake, covered in the paper, for 45 minutes. Remove the paper and bake for another 15 minutes. Check that the potatoes are cooked through by testing with the blade of a knife in the centre of the dish. If they are not quite ready, keep in the oven until they have softened sufficiently.
8. Serve warm.

CAULIFLOWER & BROCCOLI CHEESE

This simple dish with its nursery origins still delights young and old. What could be more delicious or satisfying?

Serves 8–10 as a side dish

pinch of salt
1 head of cauliflower
1 head of broccoli
75 g butter
50 g cake flour
500 ml (2 cups) milk
250 ml (1 cup) grated mature Cheddar cheese
salt and pepper

1. Fill a large saucepan about a quarter full with water. As the water will be shallow, the broccoli and cauliflower will steam rather than boil. Bring the water to the boil. Add a pinch of salt.
2. Add the cauliflower and cover with a lid. After 5 minutes, add the broccoli and cover with a lid. Cook for another 7–10 minutes until the cauliflower is cooked but not mushy and the broccoli is tender and bright green, but not overcooked.
3. Remove from the heat immediately and run under cold water to arrest the cooking process. Break up the cauliflower and broccoli into florets and scatter in a large ovenproof serving dish.
4. While the vegetables are cooking, make the cheese sauce.
5. In a medium saucepan, melt the butter and add the flour, using a wire whisk to prevent lumps. Allow the flour to cook for 30 seconds. Add the milk and, over a medium heat, stir with the whisk to avoid lumps. When the sauce starts to thicken, add the cheese and let it melt. When the cheese is melted and the sauce is thick and lovely, remove from the heat. Season with salt and pepper.
6. Pour the cheese over the cauliflower and broccoli. Serve immediately or cover with foil and keep warm in the switched off oven or warming drawer.

BAKED SWEET POTATO & PUMPKIN WITH CINNAMON, BROWN SUGAR & ORANGE

This was the first vegetable dish I learnt to make. My Uncle Pete often pulled me into Sunday lunch preparations. While stuffing the chicken and readying the trifle, he was able to give me instructions to make this simple dish, which goes well with anything. There are a variety of pumpkin and sweet potatoes available. Use whatever is available and in season.

Serves 8–10 as a side dish

700 g sweet potato, unpeeled, thickly sliced
700 g pumpkin, peeled and sliced
30 ml (2 Tbsp) treacle sugar mixed with 10 ml (2 tsp) ground cinnamon
grated orange rind (optional, but gives a wonderful flavour)
125 g butter, melted
salt and white pepper
toasted sunflower seeds, to serve

1. Preheat the oven to 180 °C.
2. Arrange the sweet potato and pumpkin in overlapping layers, alternating between the two, on a large baking tray.
3. Sprinkle over the cinnamon sugar mix and orange rind, if using. Pour over the melted butter, ensuring that the vegetables are generously coated.
4. Season with salt and pepper.
5. Cover with foil and place in the oven for 45 minutes.
6. Remove the foil and allow to crisp up slightly for another 20–30 minutes, depending on the variety of sweet potato and pumpkin used.
7. Serve hot or at room temperature, sprinkled with toasted sunflower seeds.

How to toast sunflower seeds: Preheat a small frying pan. Place 1 handful of sunflower seeds in the pan and watch closely. As the seeds brown, turn them. This happens suddenly so be careful that they don't burn. Cool completely and then store in a glass jar with a lid for up to two weeks.

SALADS

GREEN SALAD & DRESSING

Makes 1 generous cup of dressing

Basic mixture
lettuce (iceberg, cos or butter, or a combination)
cucumber, sliced
celery, sliced
spring onions, sliced (optional)

Leaves to add
rocket
watercress
baby spinach

Extras
pine nuts
walnuts, chopped
sunflower seeds
pumpkin seeds

Salad dressing
80 ml (⅓ cup) balsamic or other vinegar
salt and white pepper
5 ml (1 tsp) Dijon mustard (optional)
1 clove garlic, crushed (optional)
pinch of sugar (optional)
250 ml (1 cup) olive oil

1. Wash all the greens carefully but thoroughly. All the leaves can be placed in a sink of cold water and swirled around gently to loosen any dirt.
2. Spin the lettuce in a salad spinner or in a dry teatowel or a colander.
3. If the salad greens need to be stored before eating, place them in a covered bowl in the fridge. They can be stored like this for up to three days.
4. To serve, tear the bigger lettuce leaves into pieces (do not cut lettuce).
5. Toss in the cucumber, celery, spring onions and any other leaves you are using. Just before serving, pour over the salad dressing and toss lightly.
6. Sprinkle over any nuts or seeds you may be using.
7. To make the dressing, mix together the vinegar, salt and pepper, mustard, garlic and sugar with a wire whisk.
8. In a slow, steady stream, add the oil, whisking all the time.
9. Store in a sealed container (a jam jar works well) in the fridge and shake well before pouring over the salad.

BEETROOT & FETA SALAD

Serves 8–10

4 large beetroot
250 ml (1 cup) water
60 ml (¼ cup) sunflower seeds
30 ml (2 Tbsp) olive, sunflower or canola oil
15 ml (1 Tbsp) balsamic or red wine vinegar
½ onion or 1 bunch spring onions, very finely sliced (optional)
200 g (2 cups) feta cheese

1. Preheat the oven to 180 °C.
2. Place the beetroot, skin on, and water in a roasting pan. Cover with foil and bake for 1 hour until cooked through (a knife should cut through easily).
3. In a small saucepan or frying pan, toast the sunflower seeds in 15 ml (1 Tbsp) of the oil until lightly browned and flavourful.
4. Beat the remaining tablespoon of oil and the vinegar together in a cup to make a dressing.
5. Cut the beetroot into chunks. In a bowl, toss the beetroot chunks in the dressing. Add the onion and toasted sunflower seeds. Break the feta into chunks and mix in with the beetroot.
6. This salad will keep for three to four days, covered, in the fridge.

CABBAGE SALAD

My fabulous soul-friend Victoria brings this refreshing, crunchy salad on camping trips. Without the dressing it lasts well, so dress as you need to.

Serves 10–12

4 baby cabbages, chopped
250 g mangetout, chopped
10 spring onions, chopped
1 packet two-minute noodles (break up – don't add flavouring from the sachet)
250 ml (1 cup) slivered almonds
250 ml (1 cup) sunflower seeds
60 ml (¼ cup) white wine vinegar (sometimes I mix it with rice vinegar)
1 chicken stock cube (or powder equivalent) dissolved in 15 ml (1 Tbsp) hot water
15 ml (1 Tbsp) soy sauce
60 ml (¼ cup) sugar

1. Mix the cabbages, mangetout and spring onions together in a bowl. Roast the noodles, almonds and sunflower seeds together at 180 °C for 10 minutes until toasted and sprinkle over the cabbage mixture.
2. To make the dressing, mix the vinegar, stock, soy sauce and sugar together.
3. Add the dressing to the salad just before serving and toss to mix.

POTATO SALAD WITH MAYONNAISE

Serves 8–10

700 g potatoes (baby Mediterranean or Nicola potatoes work well)
pinch of salt
1 bunch spring onions, chopped
60 ml (¼ cup) chopped fresh parsley
250 ml (1 cup) Quick & Easy Mayonnaise (see page 170) or Hellmann's Mayonnaise
3 boiled extra-large eggs (9 minutes), chopped
2–3 gherkins, chopped (optional)
salt and pepper

1. Place the potatoes in a saucepan, cover with cold water, add a pinch of salt and bring to the boil.
2. Simmer for 20–25 minutes until the potatoes are tender right through when pricked.
3. Drain and allow to cool a little. If preferred, the potatoes can be peeled at this stage. I like to keep the skins on for texture and flavour.
4. Cut the potatoes into bite-size pieces.
5. Mix the remaining ingredients together and season to taste. Pour the mixture over the potatoes while still warm and mix gently.
6. Store, covered, in the fridge for up to four days.

POTATO SALAD WITH VINAIGRETTE

Serves 8–10

700 g potatoes (baby Mediterranean or Nicola potatoes work well)
pinch of salt
3 boiled extra-large eggs (9 minutes), chopped
30 ml (2 Tbsp) capers, drained (optional)
1 bunch spring onions, chopped
125 ml (½ cup) pitted black olives (optional)
60 ml (¼ cup) chopped fresh parsley
60 ml (¼ cup) red wine vinegar
60 ml (¼ cup) olive oil
15 ml (1 Tbsp) Dijon mustard
salt and pepper

1. Place the potatoes in a saucepan, cover with cold water, add a pinch of salt and bring to the boil.
2. Simmer for 20–25 minutes until the potatoes are tender right through when pricked.
3. Drain and allow to cool a little, then cut the potatoes into bite-size pieces. Add the eggs, capers, spring onions and olives.
4. Mix the remaining ingredients together with a wire whisk until well blended and season to taste. Pour the mixture over the potatoes while they are still warm and mix gently.
5. Serve warm or at room temperature.
6. Store, covered, in the fridge for up to four days.

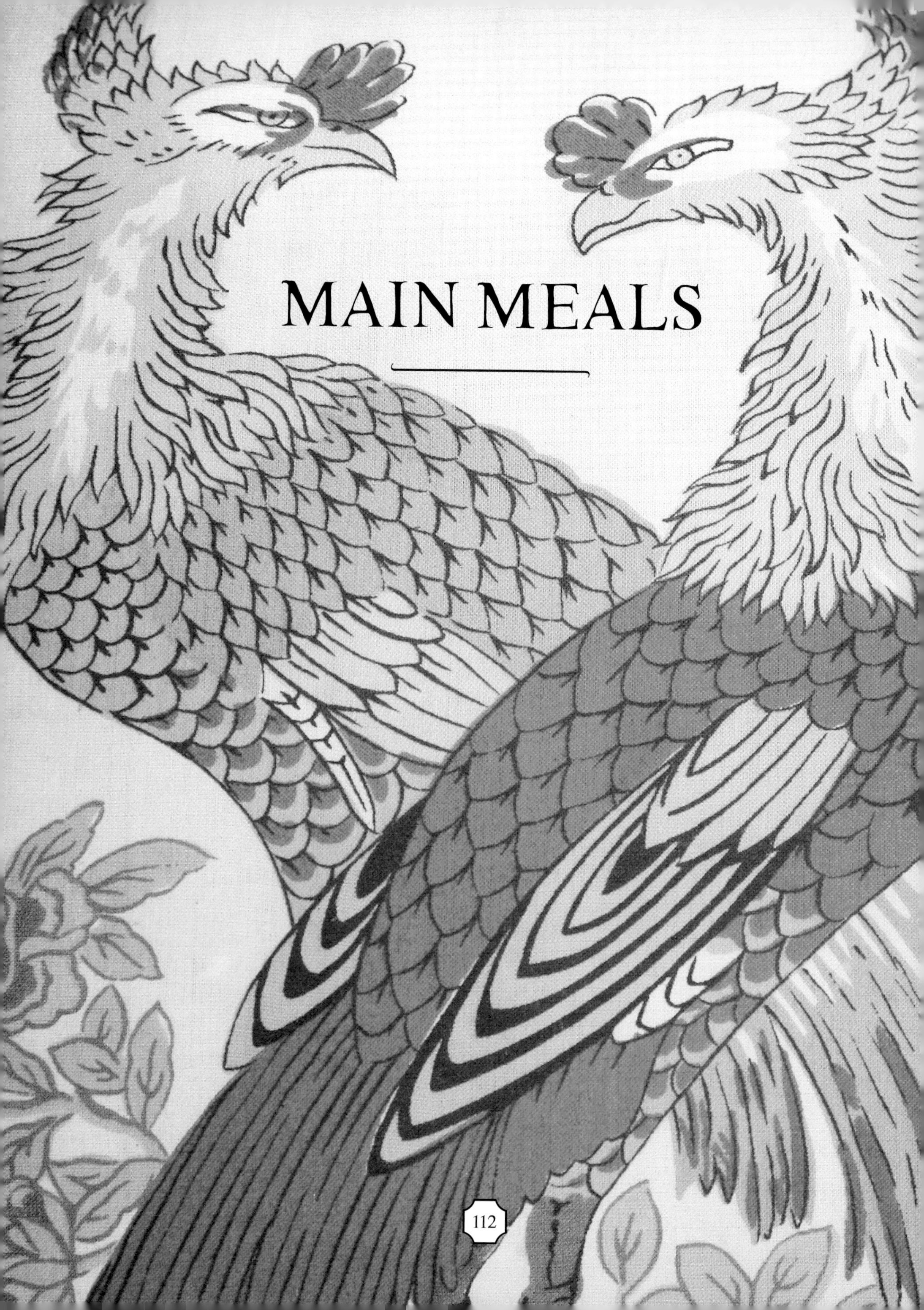

MAIN MEALS

CHICKEN

COQ AU VIN

Serves 6–8

Coq au vin is a real crowd-pleaser and I had it for the first time when my Uncle Pete cooked it for my birthday. His task was to feed 16 hungry, opinionated friends of mine in their early twenties. He carried this off, as he did with all things, with aplomb, style, much laughter and a gin and tonic in his hand. His infectious joy and ebullience went so well with this, his signature dish.

45 ml (3 Tbsp) olive oil
12 pieces chicken (drumsticks and thighs work best)
salt and pepper
1 packet streaky or back bacon, diced
500 g baby onions, pickling onions or shallots, peeled (at some supermarkets you are able to buy these already peeled and it is worth it as they can be tricky to peel)
2 onions, sliced
2 stalks celery, sliced
3 large carrots, thickly sliced
1 punnet (300 g) mushrooms, sliced (portabellini give the best flavour)
2–3 cloves garlic, crushed
750 ml (1 bottle/3 cups) red wine
250 ml (1 cup) chicken stock
5 ml (1 tsp) dried thyme or 1 handful of fresh thyme

1. Heat the oil in a large stovetop-to-oven casserole dish with a lid.
2. Brown the chicken pieces in batches, 4–5 at a time. Season with salt and pepper, and set to one side.
3. In the same casserole and oil, gently fry the bacon until just cooked through. Add all the vegetables and garlic and stir in until they are finely glazed with oil. Allow to cook gently, uncovered, for 10 minutes until their flavours develop.
4. Add the wine, turn up the heat and simmer briskly for about 10 minutes until the wine has reduced by half. Add the stock and thyme and mix in well.
5. Return the chicken pieces to the wine mixture, bring to the boil, turn down the heat, partly cover with the lid and allow to simmer for 45 minutes to 1 hour until the chicken is cooked through.

SLOW-ROASTED CHICKEN WITH LEMON, OLIVES & GARLIC

Serves 4–6

1 large free-range chicken
olive oil
15 ml (1 Tbsp) chicken stock powder
15 ml (1 Tbsp) dried mixed herbs or 1 handful of fresh thyme
sea salt and freshly ground black pepper
2 lemons
1 large head of garlic
1 packet (200 g) calamata olives

1. Preheat the oven to 160 °C.
2. Place the chicken in a roasting pan. Rub generously all over with olive oil, stock powder and herbs. Season with salt and pepper.
3. Halve the lemons and squeeze the juice all over the chicken. Stuff one half into the cavity of the chicken and scatter the other three halves around the chicken.
4. Cut the head of garlic in half, cutting across the cloves. Place the halves either side of the chicken.
5. Scatter the drained olives around the chicken.
6. Cover with foil and roast for 2 hours. For the last half hour, remove the foil so that the chicken browns and the skin crisps up.
7. Remove the chicken from the pan and carve. Strain the cooking juices through a sieve and serve in a jug with the chicken.

CHICKEN CURRY

Serves 4

45 ml (3 Tbsp) olive or sunflower oil, butter or ghee
2 onions, chopped or sliced
1 cinnamon stick
6 whole cloves
2 bay leaves
6 cardamom pods
8 chicken pieces (thighs and drumsticks)
4 potatoes, peeled and quartered
1 thumb-length piece of fresh ginger root or fresh ginger paste
1–3 cloves garlic, crushed
10 ml (2 tsp) chilli powder
5 ml (1 tsp) turmeric
10 ml (2 tsp) ground cumin
5 ml (1 tsp) ground coriander (optional)
250 ml (1 cup) plain yoghurt
salt
500 ml (2 cups) chicken stock
chopped fresh coriander and rice, to serve

1. Heat the oil in a large saucepan and fry the onions until light brown.
2. Add the cinnamon, cloves, bay leaves and cardamom and fry for 2–3 minutes.
3. Add the chicken and fry until lightly browned.
4. Add the potatoes, ginger, garlic, chilli powder, turmeric, cumin and ground coriander. Fry for 2 minutes.
5. Add the yoghurt and salt and make sure each chicken piece is coated with yoghurt. Cook, covered, for 5 minutes.
6. Add the stock and bring to the boil. Turn down the heat and simmer for 45 minutes to 1 hour.
7. Season to taste, sprinkle with chopped coriander and serve with rice.

CHICKEN PIE

Serves 8–10

2 onions, quartered
2–3 bay leaves
500 ml (2 cups) dry white wine
2 free-range chickens
salt and pepper
chicken stock powder
milk
200 g bought puff pastry, defrosted (Woolworths has a good French puff pastry)
1 extra-large egg, beaten, for glazing
potato and pea mash, to serve

SAUCE
125 g (½ cup) butter
125 ml (½ cup) cake flour
1 litre (4 cups) liquid (from chicken stock)
1 handful of frozen peas (optional)
15 ml (1 Tbsp) Dijon mustard
1 bunch spring onions, finely chopped (optional)

1. Preheat the oven to 180 °C.
2. Place the onions, bay leaves and white wine in a roasting pan. Rub the chickens with salt, pepper and stock powder and place in the roasting pan.
3. Roast for 1½ hours until the chicken is well cooked. Leave to cool.
4. Skin and debone the chicken (returning the skin and bones to the roasting pan) and strip the meat into bite-size pieces. Place the meat in a large ovenproof pie dish.
5. Add 750 ml (3 cups) boiling water to the roasting pan, scraping all the juices and brown flavour off the bottom with a wooden spoon. Simmer on the stovetop for 20 minutes. Strain through a sieve. Measure 1 litre (4 cups) of mixture made up of broth and milk.
6. To make the sauce, melt the butter in a large saucepan. Whisk in the flour. Gradually add the broth and milk mixture, stirring all the time. Once the sauce has thickened and is almost boiling, stir in the peas, mustard and spring onions and remove from the heat. Check for seasoning and add salt and pepper if necessary. Pour the sauce over the chicken and mix in gently with a spoon. Allow to cool.
7. Gently roll out the pastry as little as possible on a floured board. Lift the pastry and place on top of the chicken dish, leaving the sides hanging over. (The pie can be frozen at this point.)
8. Preheat the oven to 220 °C.
9. Brush with a beaten egg and cut a criss-cross pattern in the pastry with the back of a knife.
10. Bake for 40 minutes until well browned and puffed up.
11. Serve hot with a potato and pea mash.

CHUTNEY CHICKEN

Purists will be horrified that I have included this recipe. Quick, easy and immensely satisfying, this was a staple on our family menu growing up. Now, as a working mother myself, I understand why my mother fell back on it so often. Hide the packet soup away from your idealistic friends, but do make it for them. Just make sure you make enough. Served with brown rice and a green salad, this delicious meal couldn't be easier.

Serves 6–8

12 chicken thighs and drumsticks or assorted chicken pieces
250 ml (1 cup) chutney (Mrs Ball's is still my favourite)
250 ml (1 cup) freshly squeezed orange juice
1 packet brown onion soup powder
fresh coriander leaves (optional)
cucumber, cut into sticks (optional)

1. Preheat the oven to 180 °C.
2. Place the chicken pieces on a baking tray or in casserole dish. The chicken pieces should not be too snug. Some space in between them allows them to roast and develop a lovely sticky coating.
3. Mix the chutney, orange juice and onion soup together. Pour over the chicken pieces.
4. Roast for 45 minutes until browned all over and the liquid has reduced to a lovely, gooey sauce.
5. Serve hot or at room temperature.
6. Garnish with finely chopped or whole coriander leaves and/or cucumber sticks.

CHICKEN MARBELLA

I have adapted this recipe from the wonderful American classic *The Silver Palate Cookbook*. I have reduced the sugar, added one or two ingredients and made it suitable for South African weights and measurements. This easy-to-make and delicious dish is unparalleled when it comes to feeding a crowd. It never fails to draw gasps of admiration.

Serves 8–10

16 pieces chicken (drumsticks and thighs)
100 g cloves garlic, puréed
60 ml (¼ cup) dried origanum
salt and black pepper
125 ml (½ cup) red wine vinegar
125 ml (½ cup) olive oil
250 ml (1 cup) pitted prunes
1 packet (200 g) green olives, pitted and drained
125 ml (½ cup) capers, with a bit of juice
6 bay leaves
45 ml (3 Tbsp) dark brown sugar
chicken stock powder for sprinkling
250 ml (1 cup) dry white wine
chopped fresh parsley or coriander, or combination of fresh herbs, to serve

1. In a large bowl with a lid or covered in plastic wrap, marinate the chicken with the garlic, origanum, salt, pepper, vinegar, olive oil, prunes, olives, capers and bay leaves overnight or for at least 8 hours.
2. Preheat the oven to 180 °C.
3. Arrange the chicken pieces in two large roasting pans and pour over the marinade. I use my iron casserole serving dishes as there is less washing up.
4. Sprinkle the chicken pieces with sugar and chicken stock powder. Season lightly with salt and pepper. Gently pour over the wine.
5. Roast for 1 hour until the chicken has browned nicely and a lovely sauce has developed from the pan juices and wine.
6. Serve sprinkled with chopped herbs.

ROAST CHICKEN & VEGETABLES

Serves 6

1 large chicken (preferably free-range or grain-fed)
45 ml (3 Tbsp) extra virgin olive oil (or other oil)
15 ml (1 Tbsp) chicken stock powder
5 ml (1 tsp) dried mixed herbs (or 1 handful of fresh rosemary and thyme picked from the garden, washed and finely chopped)
sea salt (or table salt) and black pepper
1 lemon (optional)
4 large potatoes with jackets left on or 4 potatoes peeled and quartered
4 large carrots
1 butternut, cut up (skin on or off according to taste) or 1 packet cubed butternut

1. Preheat the oven to 180 °C.
2. Place the chicken in a roasting pan.
3. Rub the chicken with 15 ml (1 Tbsp) of the oil, the stock powder, mixed herbs, salt and pepper.
4. Roll the lemon on a hard surface to soften it slightly. Prick through the skin 15–20 times and stuff the lemon into the cavity of the chicken.
5. Rub the remaining oil and salt over all the vegetables. Arrange the vegetables around the chicken in the roasting pan.
6. Place in the oven and roast for 1½ hours.
7. Once the chicken is roasted, strain the roasting juices and serve as gravy.

Tip: Any leftover chicken can be used cold, mixed with mayonnaise, as a sandwich filling the next day.

BEEF & LAMB

OXTAIL

Serves 6

1,5 kg oxtail pieces
125 ml (½ cup) flour in a plastic bag mixed with 5 ml (1 tsp) mustard powder, 5 ml (1 tsp) salt and 2,5 ml (½ tsp) white pepper
30 ml (2 Tbsp) olive oil
2 onions, finely sliced or chopped
2 stalks celery, sliced
5 ml (1 tsp) dried mixed herbs
2 carrots, thickly sliced
15 ml (1 Tbsp) tomato paste
1 tin (410 g) tomatoes
5 ml (1 tsp) sugar
500 ml (2 cups) red wine (replace with stock if preferred)
750 ml (3 cups) beef stock
2 bay leaves
potato or sweet potato mash, to serve

1. Preheat the oven to 100 °C.
2. Place the oxtail pieces (3–4 at a time) in the plastic bag and shake to coat well with the floury mixture.
3. Heat the oil in a large stovetop-to-oven casserole dish with a lid.
4. Brown the oxtail pieces, a few at a time, until well browned. Remove from the casserole with a slotted spoon and keep aside.
5. Add the onions, celery and mixed herbs to the casserole and cook gently until starting to brown.
6. Add the carrots and simmer for 5 minutes.
7. Add the tomato paste, the tinned tomatoes and the sugar and simmer for another minute or so.
8. Add the red wine and turn up the heat so that the mixture is bubbling fast and the wine reduces by half.
9. Add the beef stock and bay leaves and bring to a brisk simmer.
10. Return the browned oxtail pieces to the casserole, put the lid on and place the casserole in the oven.
11. Allow the oxtail to cook for at least 8 hours until the meat is soft and falling off the bone.
12. Serve with potato or sweet potato mash.

ROAST BEEF & YORKSHIRE PUDDING

When roasting it is essential to preheat the oven, keep an eye on time, allow the joint to rest before carving and to use the best quality ingredients at your disposal.

Serves 8

Roast Beef

1 beef roast (2,5 kg)
30 ml (2 Tbsp) cake flour mixed with 15 ml (1 Tbsp) English mustard powder (for the beef)
10 ml (2 tsp) salt
5 ml (1 tsp) white pepper
1 generous bunch of fresh thyme
mustard and/or horseradish sauce, to serve

Yorkshire pudding

2 extra-large eggs
250 ml (1 cup) milk
250 ml (1 cup) cake flour
pinch of salt
60–75 ml (4–5 Tbsp) canola oil

Gravy

30 ml (2 Tbsp) cake flour
500 ml (2 cups) beef stock (or 125 ml [½ cup] red wine and 375 ml [1½ cups] beef stock)

1. Preheat the oven to 200 °C.
2. Pat the beef roast dry and rub with the flour and mustard powder mixture. Season with the salt and pepper.
3. Place the joint on the bunch of thyme in a roasting pan, with the fatty side uppermost.
4. Roast the meat for 15 minutes per 500 g (for a standard joint of 2,5 kg, this will take 1¼ hours). The meat should be medium pink in the middle. If you prefer medium-rare, reduce the cooking time; if you prefer well done, increase the cooking time.
5. Remove from the oven and allow to rest on a carving board, covered in foil.
6. While the beef is cooking, make the Yorkshire pudding. Using a wire whisk and a jug or small bowl mix the eggs, milk and cake flour together. Add the salt.
7. Spoon the oil into a 12-cup muffin pan and place in the oven about 15 minutes before you expect the joint to be cooked.
8. Once the roast is removed from the oven, pour the Yorkshire pudding mixture into the heated muffin pan and return to the oven. Bake for 15–20 minutes until well risen and browned.
9. To make the gravy, discard the thyme from the roasting pan and return the pan, with the pan juices, to the stovetop. Heat and scatter over the flour. Using a wire whisk, mix the pan juices and the flour to a paste.
10. Gradually add the stock, stirring well with a wire whisk. Allow to come to the boil and thicken. Season to taste. Pour the gravy into a warmed jug.
11. Carve the beef into thin slices and serve with the Yorkshire pudding, gravy, mustard and/or horseradish sauce.

FILLET WITH BÉARNAISE SAUCE

Serves 8–10

1 large fillet
mustard powder or Dijon mustard
pepper
60 g (¼ cup) butter
60 ml (¼ cup) olive oil

Sauce
60 ml (¼ cup) tarragon vinegar
60 ml (¼ cup) dry white wine
3 extra-large egg yolks
1 spring onion, finely chopped
pinch each of salt and pepper
250 ml (1 cup) melted butter

1. Preheat the oven to 180 °C.
2. Rub the fillet all over with mustard powder (or Dijon mustard) and pepper.
3. In a large stovetop-to-oven casserole dish or roasting pan, melt the butter and oil on top of the stove. Brown the fillet all over (turning only once). It should be a good dark brown, but not cooked through (about 10 minutes).
4. Place the fillet in the oven and cook for a further 15–20 minutes (according to taste).
5. To make the béarnaise sauce, place the vinegar and white wine in a small saucepan and reduce, uncovered, over high heat until there is about 60 ml (¼ cup)or 4 Tbsp left.
6. Place the egg yolks, spring onion, salt, pepper and vinegar mixture in the bowl of a food processor and blend very well. Heat the butter to boiling point (in a jug in a microwave or another small saucepan) and then trickle in a steady stream into the egg and vinegar mixture, blending all the time. Pour into a warmed jug and leave in a warm (not hot) place. (If the béarnaise is stored in the fridge, it firms up and becomes more like a tarragon mayonnaise and is just as delicious cold.)
7. Remove the fillet from the oven, cover with foil or a teatowel and leave in a warm (not hot) place to rest. Carve after 5–10 minutes and serve on hot plates with the béarnaise sauce, or cool completely and serve at room temperature.

BOLOGNAISE-STYLE MINCE FOR COTTAGE PIE & LASAGNE

This recipe can be doubled to make large quantities or for freezing.

Serves 6

500 g beef mince
10 ml (2 tsp) olive oil or other oil
1 packet bacon, diced (optional)
1 onion, chopped
1 clove garlic
2 stalks celery (optional)
3 carrots, peeled and grated (optional)
15 ml (1 Tbsp) dried mixed herbs
1 tin (85 g) tomato paste
1 tin (410 g) tomatoes
250 ml (1 cup) red wine
500 ml (2 cups) chicken or beef stock (I like to use beef for a fuller flavour)
salt and pepper

1. Preheat the oven to 160 °C.
2. In a large saucepan, gently fry the mince in the oil until well browned, using a fork to separate it. If using bacon, which adds a lovely intense flavour, cook it first, before the mince. Add the mince directly to the cooked bacon.
3. Add the onion and garlic, and fry gently for 5 minutes until the onion is soft.
4. Add the celery, carrots and mixed herbs and continue frying for 3 minutes until the celery is pale.
5. Add the tomato paste and tinned tomatoes and mix in well with a wooden spoon.
6. Add the wine and cook briskly for about 5 minutes so that it reduces.
7. Add the stock, season to taste with the salt and pepper, and leave to simmer over low heat with the lid half on, on top of the stove, for 1 hour.

Tips:

~ I prefer to use the oven to develop a good flavour. To finish in the oven, place the saucepan with the lid on, in a preheated oven of 160 °C for 1½ hours.
~ Add a tin of beans (borlotti or kidney) in the last 30 minutes of cooking.
~ Cheat's cottage pie: Spoon the mince mixture into an ovenproof dish, cover with mashed potatoes and grill until golden brown. If I make this mince for cottage pie only, I leave out the tinned tomatoes and wine and use beef stock. This is a beefier and less saucey version.
~ Serve with pasta and grated Parmesan cheese as a bolognaise sauce.
~ Lasagne: Layer the mince mixture in a serving dish with pasta sheets and white sauce (made with 125 g butter, 125 ml (½ cup) cake flour, 1 litre (4 cups) milk, nutmeg, salt and pepper). Top with white sauce and sprinkle over Parmesan cheese. Bake at 180 °C for 45 minutes. Allow to stand before serving.

MEATBALLS

Serves 8–10

A standard favourite for school lunches, picnics and road trips, meatballs are a versatile and portable meal. To turn this recipe into meatballs in tomato sauce, use the Basic Tomato Sauce recipe on page 168 and double it.

1 kg mince (I like to use a combination of beef, lamb and/or pork when available)
1 onion
5 ml (1 tsp) ground cumin
5 ml (1 tsp) ground cinnamon
2 medium-sized carrots, grated
60 ml (¼ cup) chopped fresh parsley (if you have it)
5 ml (1 tsp) salt
pinch of white pepper
45 ml (3 Tbsp) olive oil

1. Using your hands, mix all the ingredients, except the oil, together until well mixed.
2. Shape into approximately 40 balls with your hands.
3. Heat the oil in a shallow frying pan and gently fry the meatballs, 10 at a time, until browned all over and cooked through.
4. If adding the tomato sauce, return all the meatballs to the frying pan and pour over the sauce. Warm up before serving.

BOBOTIE

Serves 8–10

My favourite bobotie recipe is uncomplicated, authentic and covered in a thin layer of finely flaked almonds. This ultimate South African classic, followed by malva pudding or milk tart, takes comfort food to its high point.

1 kg beef mince (lean, not extra-lean as it can become too dry)
50 ml canola or olive oil
2 onions, chopped
2 cloves garlic
10 ml (2 tsp) salt
5 ml (1 tsp) white pepper
450 ml (1¾ cups) beef stock
60 ml (¼ cup) chutney
60 ml (¼ cup) tomato paste
15 ml (1 Tbsp) apricot jam
20 ml (4 tsp) vinegar
60 ml (¼ cup) sultanas (optional)
30 ml (2 Tbsp) curry powder (strength to your taste)
2 slices white bread, soaked in a little milk
2 bananas, mashed

TOPPING
2 extra-large eggs
250 ml (1 cup) milk
pinch of salt
100 g (1 cup) flaked almonds
2–3 bay leaves

1. Preheat the oven to 150 °C.
2. In a large casserole dish or saucepan, brown the mince very well in the oil.
3. Add the onions and garlic and cook gently for about 10 minutes until the onions are transparent.
4. Add the salt, pepper and stock.
5. Lower the heat and simmer gently, semi-covered, for 30 minutes.
6. Add the chutney, tomato paste, apricot jam, vinegar, sultanas and curry powder and stir well to distribute the flavours.
7. Allow to cook gently for another 10 minutes.
8. Remove from the heat. Squeeze the milk out of the bread and mash with the bananas. Add to the mince mixture and stir in well.
9. Place the mince mixture in an ovenproof dish.
10. For the topping, whisk the eggs, milk and salt together in a small bowl and carefully pour over the mince mixture.
11. Scatter over a layer of flaked almonds and dot the bay leaves here and there.
12. Bake for 35–40 minutes until set and just starting to brown on top.

BREDIE
(chicken, beef or lamb)

Serves 4–6

8 pieces chicken (thighs and drumsticks)
OR
800 g–1 kg cubed beef
OR
800 g–1 kg cubed lamb (can have a bit of bone, e.g. knuckles or stewing lamb)

30 ml (2 Tbsp) olive oil
salt and pepper
1 onion, chopped
1–3 cloves garlic, finely chopped
2 carrots, sliced
1 tin (410 g) whole Italian tomatoes
1 tin (85 g) tomato paste
10 ml (2 tsp) dried mixed herbs
250 ml (1 cup) chicken stock
4 potatoes, sliced
basmati, brown or white rice, to serve

1. In a heavy-bottomed saucepan, fry the chicken/beef/lamb in batches in the olive oil until brown. Remove the browned meat from the saucepan and keep on a plate. Season the meat with salt and pepper.
2. In the same saucepan, gently brown the onion and garlic over medium heat. Add the carrots and cook for 2 minutes.
3. Add the tomatoes, tomato paste, mixed herbs and chicken stock.
4. Return the meat to the saucepan and bring to the boil.
5. Simmer gently for 1 hour with the lid half on.
6. Add the sliced potatoes and simmer for another 30 minutes with the lid off.
7. Serve with basmati, brown or white rice.

SLOW-COOKED LAMB

The joy in this recipe is being able to pop everything in the oven before I leave for work in the morning, and coming home to delicious smells and one of the best meals I know. It takes all the pain out of entertaining. Seriously impressive, this couldn't be easier. Don't be tempted to fuss over it and open the lid; leave the flavours to develop all on their own.

Serves 8–10

45 ml (3 Tbsp) olive oil
2 onions, sliced
1 large head of garlic, halved horizontally
250 ml (1 cup) red wine
250 ml (1 cup) chicken stock
3 or 4 sprigs fresh rosemary
1 medium-sized leg of lamb (2,5–3 kg)
salt and pepper

1. Preheat the oven to 120 °C.
2. Rub a casserole dish (with a lid) with a little of the olive oil. Place the onions, garlic, red wine, chicken stock and rosemary into the dish. Place the lamb on top and rub the lamb all over with olive oil, salt and pepper.
3. Run baking paper under the tap, wring it out and place on top of the lamb.
4. Cover the dish with the lid and place in the oven for 10 hours. Do not open the lid during this time.
5. To serve, remove the baking paper, spoon the cooking juices over the lamb, and spoon the meat off the bone, giving each serving generous amounts of garlic and juice. Serve very simply with crusty bread and a green salad or green beans.

PORK

SLOW-COOKED PORK NECK ON A BED OF APPLES & ONIONS

Pork belly is easier to find than neck, but it can be very fatty and because of the slow, covered cooking process, you may end up with too much fat. Look for the neck or ask your supermarket or butcher to prepare it for you. It has an excellent flavour and responds well to slow cooking.

Serves 6–8

1 rolled pork neck (around 2 kg)
30 ml (2 Tbsp) olive oil
6 apples (Granny Smith gives good flavour), cored and quartered but not peeled
2 onions, sliced
1 handful of fresh sage leaves
500 ml (2 cups) dry white wine or dry cider (apple cider is delicious if you can get it)
30 ml (2 Tbsp) English mustard
salt and white pepper
mashed potatoes and sautéed cabbage, to serve

1. Preheat the oven to 140 °C.
2. In a heavy-bottomed stovetop-to-oven casserole dish with a lid, brown the pork on all sides in the olive oil.
3. Remove from the heat and remove the pork from the dish.
4. Place the apples, onions and sage leaves in the bottom of the casserole dish and put the pork back on top. Pour over the wine or cider, rub the pork with mustard and season the whole dish with salt and pepper.
5. Place a piece of wet, wrung out baking paper or old butter wrapper on the pork and tuck it down loosely. This helps keep the meat juicy. Cover the dish with the lid.
6. Roast for 2½–3 hours until very soft and flavourful.
7. Serve with mashed potatoes and sautéed cabbage, Savoy if you can find it.

SEAFOOD

Right: Paella, recipe on page 156

PAELLA

A celebration dish, paella is fun and easy to make. If finishing in the oven in a covered casserole dish, much of the work can be done ahead of time. Try to have all the ingredients washed and sliced or diced ahead of time. If being made in a skottel, the process takes about 1½ hours. Get the whole family involved.

Serves 12 generously

15 ml (1 Tbsp) butter
30 ml (2 Tbsp) olive oil
300 g chorizo sausage
12 chicken pieces
chicken stock powder, for sprinkling
salt and pepper
60 ml (¼ cup) water
3 onions (red ones if you can find them), thinly sliced
3–4 cloves garlic, chopped
2 tins (410 g each) chopped Italian tomatoes
3 mixed peppers (red and yellow), sliced
pinch of brown sugar
2,5 ml (½ tsp) cayenne pepper
10 ml (2 tsp) paprika
pinch of saffron or turmeric
500 g white rice (risotto, paella or regular white rice)
250 ml (1 cup) dry white wine (if not using wine, substitute with extra chicken stock)
500–750 ml (2–3 cups) warm chicken stock, kept on one side in a jug
250 ml (1 cup) pitted black olives
1 handful of frozen peas
500 g mixed seafood (mussels, calamari, fish) – use the best you can afford and, if frozen, defrost before cooking
12–16 defrosted prawns, deveined (if preferred, 750 g frozen prawn meat can be used)
125 ml (½ cup) chopped fresh parsley
1–2 lemons, cut attractively, to serve

1. In a large stovetop-to-oven casserole dish, frying pan with a lid or in the skottel, melt the butter and olive oil. Add the chorizo and fry gently for a couple of minutes. Remove from the heat and set aside.
2. Sprinkle the chicken pieces with the chicken stock powder, salt and pepper and brown all over in batches. Once all the pieces are browned, return them all to the dish. Add the water, cover with a lid and allow to cook through for 20–25 minutes. Remove the chicken from the dish and set aside.
3. Add the onions and garlic to the dish and fry gently until transparent and flavourful. Add the tomatoes and peppers and fry gently until wilted and flavourful.
4. Season with sugar, cayenne pepper, paprika and saffron.
5. Add the rice and mix in with a wooden spoon, making sure all the rice grains are well covered with the tomato and onion mixture.
6. Turn up the heat and add the wine. Allow the wine to cook off for 5–10 minutes.
7. Add the chicken stock, chicken pieces and chorizo, mix well, turn down the heat and cover. Simmer for about 15 minutes until the rice is just cooked and most of the liquid has been absorbed. Don't overcook at this stage as the paella continues cooking and the rice will become mushy.
8. If not using a skottel, preheat the oven to 180 °C.
9. Once the rice is cooked and plumped up, scatter over the olives, peas and seafood. Replace the lid and cook through (in the oven or on the skottel) for another 5–10 minutes. The prawns should just turn pink and the peas should be defrosted. The rice should plumped up and cooked through.
10. Turn down the heat, fork the chopped parsley through the rice and serve immediately with lemon wedges.

CONDIMENTS

BASIL PESTO

Makes scant cup

500 ml (2 cups) fresh basil leaves
80 ml (⅓ cup) pine nuts
1–4 cloves garlic, depending on taste
125 ml (½ cup) good quality grated
Parmesan cheese
125 ml (½ cup) olive oil
salt and black pepper

1. Using a food processor or handheld blender, process the basil leaves, pine nuts, garlic and cheese until mixed but not smooth.
2. With the blade running, gradually pour in the olive oil until the mixture becomes a thick paste/pesto.
3. Season to taste with salt and pepper.
4. If the pesto is not to be eaten immediately, store in a glass jar with a lid in the fridge for up to two weeks. Pour a thin layer of olive oil on top of the pesto once it is in the jar, to seal it and prevent the basil from blackening.

HUMMUS

Makes a generous cup

- 1 tin (410 g) chickpeas or 190 ml (¾ cup) dried chickpeas, soaked overnight
- juice of 1 lemon
- 45 ml (3 Tbsp) tahini (sesame paste) (optional)
- 2 cloves garlic, finely chopped
- pinch of cumin
- salt and pepper
- olive oil
- paprika

1. If using dried, soaked chickpeas, place in a saucepan, cover generously with water, bring to the boil and simmer for 1½ hours until very soft (keep the cooking water). Alternatively, use drained tinned chickpeas (keep the drained water).
2. In a food processor or with a handheld blender, blend the chickpeas with the lemon juice, tahini, garlic and cumin.
3. Season with salt and pepper.
4. Place in a serving bowl and brush the top with olive oil to prevent it drying out. Sprinkle with paprika. Store in an airtight container in the fridge for up to one week unopened.

CHICKEN LIVER PÂTÉ

Makes 2 generous cups

30 ml (2 Tbsp) butter
2 onions, finely sliced
2 cloves garlic, finely chopped
500 g chicken livers, defrosted
30 ml (2 Tbsp) brandy or sherry (or chicken stock if preferred)
10 ml (2 tsp) dried mixed herbs
5 ml (1 tsp) salt
pinch each of pepper and nutmeg
fresh herbs, e.g. Italian flat-leaf parsley or sage, for garnishing
extra 100 g butter, melted, for topping

1. Heat the 30 ml (2 Tbsp) butter in a frying pan.
2. Add the onions and garlic and cook gently for 10 minutes until transparent and aromatic.
3. Add the chicken livers and cook for a couple of minutes on each side. Do not overcook. They should be lightly browned but still a little pink in the middle.
4. Add the brandy, herbs, salt, pepper and nutmeg. Simmer for a couple of minutes.
5. Transfer to a food processor and blend until smooth.
6. Pack the pâté into one serving dish or individual ramekins and smooth over.
7. Place a leaf of parsley or sage on top of the pâté and pour over the melted butter in a thin layer.
8. Allow to cool and serve chilled.

TARTARE SAUCE

Makes 1 generous cup

250 ml (1 cup) Quick & Easy Mayonnaise (see page 170 OR Hellman's if you prefer a classic mayonnaise, Cross & Blackwell if you prefer a tangy mayonnaise)
10 ml (2 tsp) capers
2 large gherkins, finely diced
salt and pepper
chopped fresh parsley

1. Mix all the ingredients together gently and store in a cool place for up to two weeks.
2. Serve with fish, chicken or anything that needs a bit of perking up.

BASIC TOMATO SAUCE

Use as a base sauce or a pasta sauce.

Makes 1½ cups

1 onion, chopped
1–3 cloves garlic, sliced
15 ml (1 Tbsp) olive oil
2 carrots, chopped or sliced
2 stalks celery, chopped
1 handful of fresh parsley or basil or a mixture of both OR if using dried herbs, use 5 ml (1 tsp) mixed herbs, origanum or basil or a mixture
2 tins (410 g each) Italian tomatoes
5 ml (1 tsp) brown sugar
salt and pepper

1. In a saucepan, gently fry the onion and garlic in the olive oil.
2. Add the carrots and celery and sauté for another few minutes.
3. Add the herbs, the tomatoes and the brown sugar and simmer gently for 30 minutes.
4. Season to taste.

TIPS:

~ For a smooth sauce, strain through a sieve or purée in a blender.
~ For a change of flavour, add olives, capers, tinned artichokes or a couple of anchovies.

QUICK & EASY MAYONNAISE

Elizabeth David remarked that as much mayonnaise as is put out is used. This recipe may not be classic or purist, but it never fails and is delicious. A food processor or handheld blender is a must.

Makes 400 ml (1³⁄₅ cups)

2 extra-large eggs (grain-fed give the best colour)
60 ml (¼ cup) apple cider vinegar or red wine vinegar
5 ml (1 tsp) salt
2,5 ml (½ tsp) white pepper
10 ml (2 tsp) English or Dijon mustard
pinch of mixed dried herbs or 10 ml (2 tsp) chopped fresh herbs (optional)
250 ml (1 cup) extra virgin olive oil mixed with 250 ml (1 cup) canola oil

1. Place the eggs, vinegar, salt, pepper, mustard and herbs into the food processor and blend for 1 minute.
2. Gradually, in a thin trickle, add the oil.
3. Store in a glass jar in the fridge for up to one month.

BAKING & PUDDINGS

2 ML 1/2 TEASPOON

BAKING

FARM BREAD

A slice of hot homemade bread with butter must be up there with the best treats. Easy to make, the trick is in the flour and in the kneading. Bread flour, particularly stone ground, delivers the best results and a lovely crust. I have also used cake flour when it was the only one available, and it was fine, only softer.

Makes 2 loaves

1 kg bread flour (I like to mix half brown and half white)
1 packet (10 g) instant yeast
20 ml (4 tsp) salt
10 ml (2 tsp) sugar
600 ml (2 ⅖ cups) warm water
30 ml (2 Tbsp) olive oil

1. In a large mixing bowl, mix together the flour, yeast, salt and sugar.
2. Add the water and olive oil and mix in well.
3. Using the dough hook on your mixer or your hands on a floured surface, knead the dough very well, until smooth and elastic (5 minutes in a mixer, 10 minutes by hand).
4. Leave the dough to rise in a warm place in the mixing bowl, covered by a damp teatowel. A warming drawer or a sunny spot out of the wind is ideal. Depending on the warmth, this can take anything from 30 minutes to 1 hour. The dough should be doubled in size.
5. Punch the dough down with your fist and knead again until the dough is smooth.
6. Preheat the oven to 220 °C. Butter two loaf tins generously.
7. Divide the dough in two and shape to fit into the loaf tins.
8. Leave to rise for a further 20 minutes until well risen again.
9. Bake for 40–45 minutes until nicely browned. To check that the loaf is cooked through, knock it out of the tin, turn it over and, when tapped, the bread should sound hollow. If the sound is a dull thud, take it out of the tin and return to the oven for a couple of minutes to crisp up properly.
10. I like to rub the loaf with a butter wrapper (see page 15) while it is still hot. This gives the bread a glaze and softens the crust a little.

LINDSAY'S QUICK & EASY SEED LOAF

This recipe was given to me by a beloved friend decades ago. It is so good and so easy that I used it as the first lesson of the cooking courses I used to run. It is especially delicious toasted.

Makes 1 loaf

600 ml (2⅖ cups) buttermilk or plain yoghurt
750 ml (3 cups) wholewheat flour
250 ml (1 cup) oats
60 ml (¼ cup) sunflower seeds
45 ml (3 Tbsp) sesame seeds
15 ml (1 Tbsp) poppy seeds
2,5 ml (½ tsp) salt
10 ml (2 tsp) brown sugar
10 ml (2 tsp) bicarbonate of soda

1. Preheat the oven to 180 °C. Grease and flour a loaf tin.
2. Mix all the ingredients together in a bowl.
3. Place the mixture in the loaf tin and bake for 1 hour. The loaf should be firm to the touch, well risen and browned.
4. Turn the bread out of the tin. It should sound hollow when tapped underneath. This ensures a crispier crust. Place the loaf back in the oven (out of the tin) and switch off the oven. Leave it for 15–20 minutes in the oven while it cools down.
5. Allow to cool a bit before slicing.

BANANA BREAD

We always seem to have two or three bananas that don't get eaten before they turn black. I looked all over for the best banana bread recipe and found it in Jane Hornby's *What to Cook and How to Cook It*. I prefer to leave banana bread un-iced as slices sandwiched together with butter are lovely for school lunches.

Makes 1 loaf

3 ripe or very ripe bananas (the riper the banana, the better the flavour)
120 g butter, at room temperature
120 g brown or treacle sugar
2,5 ml (½ tsp) salt
3 extra-large eggs
5 ml (1 tsp) vanilla essence
100 g cake flour
120 g wholewheat flour
10 ml (2 tsp) baking powder
50 g chopped walnuts (optional)

1. Preheat the oven to 160 °C. Grease or spray a loaf tin.
2. Mash the bananas with a fork on a flat plate.
3. Mix all the ingredients together in a mixing bowl.
4. Pour the mixture into the prepared tin.
5. Bake for 1 hour and 10 minutes until well risen and golden brown.
6. Allow to cool slightly before turning out onto a cooling rack.
7. Serve immediately or store wrapped in greaseproof paper for 3–4 days.

STAINLESS STEEL

BUTTERMILK RUSKS

Makes 72

My cousin Coral, one of the best cooks I know, gave me her rusk recipe. She dries her rusks in a warming drawer but since I don't have one, I dry them overnight in the oven at around 100 °C. These rusks are foolproof, relatively healthy and everyone seems to love them.

450 g butter
500 ml (2 cups) brown sugar
2 extra-large eggs
500 ml (2 cups) buttermilk
5 ml (1 tsp) salt
1 kg self-raising flour
10 ml (2 tsp) baking powder
500 ml (2 cups) sunflower seeds
500 ml (2 cups) oats
625 ml (2½ cups) All-bran Flakes

1. Preheat the oven to 180 °C. Grease and line a roasting pan with baking paper.
2. In a very large saucepan, melt the butter and brown sugar together. If you don't have a large saucepan, melt the butter and sugar together in batches in a microwave oven and then transfer into a large mixing bowl.
3. Add the eggs, one by one.
4. Add the buttermilk.
5. Add all the dry ingredients.
6. Mix well (I have from time to time put all the ingredients in the mixer, but mixing with a large spoon in a roomy bowl gives a more rustic, crusty rusk, which I prefer) and press into the roasting pan.
7. Bake for 1 hour .
8. Remove from the oven and allow to cool a bit. Cut into rusks, separate, move onto baking trays and allow to dry in the oven overnight or for 6–8 hours at 100 °C.
9. Store in an airtight container.

Kellogg's
PEP
BRAN FLAKES
WHEAT

RIGHT: Gogo van der Riet's Christmas cake, recipe on page 186

GOGO VAN DER RIET'S CHRISTMAS CAKE

There is a lovely road that runs from Ixopo into the hills. These hills are grass-covered and rolling, and they are lovely beyond any singing of it. The road climbs seven miles into them, to Carisbrooke; and from there, if there is no mist, you look down on one of the fairest valleys of Africa. About you there is grass and bracken and you may hear the forlorn crying of the titihoya, one of the birds of the veld. Below you is the valley of the Umzimkulu, on its journey from the Drakensberg to the sea; and beyond and behind the river, great hill after great hill; and beyond and behind them, the mountains of Ingeli and East Griqualand.

The grass is rich and matted, you cannot see the soil. It holds the rain and the mist, and they seep into the ground, feeding the streams in every kloof. It is well-tended, and not too many cattle feed upon it; not too many fires burn it, laying bare the soil. Stand unshod upon it, for the ground is holy, being even as it came from the Creator. Keep it, guard it, care for it, for it keeps men, guards men, cares for men. Destroy it and man is destroyed.

Alan Paton, *Cry the Beloved Country*

I was born into a small farming community outside Kokstad in East Griquland. Even though I left there when I was four years old, it remains my heart place. My godmother, Ingie Bryden, is central to my childhood and food memories. Here is her grandmother's excellent fruit cake recipe.

Makes 1 generous cake

500 g currants
500 g sultanas
250 g raisins
250 g candied peel
250 g glacé cherries
125 ml (½ cup) brandy
250 g blanched or slivered almonds
250 g (1 cup) butter, at room temperature
300 g sugar
5 ml (1 tsp) vanilla essence
5 ml (1 tsp) almond essence
4 extra-large eggs
500 g cake flour
15 ml (1 Tbsp) ground mixed spice
10 ml (2 tsp) ground cinnamon
pinch of salt
125 ml (½ cup) marmalade or apricot jam
5 ml (1 tsp) bicarbonate of soda dissolved in 15 ml (1 Tbsp) milk

1. Pour boiling water over all the fruit, drain and then soak in the brandy overnight.
2. Preheat the oven to 160 °C. Grease and double line a large cake tin.
3. Roast the almonds on a baking tray in the oven until just browned. Chop.
4. In a large mixing bowl, cream the butter and sugar together well.
5. Add the vanilla and almond essences and the eggs, one at a time, beating well in between.
6. Sift in the flour, spices and salt and fold in.
7. Mix in the marmalade or jam, fruit, brandy and nuts.
8. Add the bicarbonate of soda and milk.
9. Pour the mixture into the prepared cake tin and cover with foil.
10. Bake for 2 hours at 180 °C and then reduce the heat to 140 °C and bake for a further 4 hours.
11. Allow to cool completely in the tin and store wrapped in greaseproof paper and foil.

DIANA'S CHOCOLATE CAKE

My mother's name was Diana. She always served this chocolate cake filled with homemade strawberry or apricot jam, and slathered in butter icing. Ina Paarman has the same recipe in *Cook with Ina Paarman*, coincidentally named after another Diana. Both Dianas knew what they were up to – this is a foolproof, moist, deeply chocolatey crowd-pleasing winner of a cake. I have added vanilla essence to the mixture, upped the cocoa and I often fill it with caramel treat and ice with the Butter Icing on page 200. If you like your icing to be generous, double the icing recipe.

Serves 12–18, depending on size of slices. If baked in a roasting pan or lined beer box (school birthdays), it can be cut into 24.

500 ml (2 cups) sugar
250 ml (1 cup) canola oil
250 ml (1 cup) warm water
6 extra-large eggs, separated
5 ml (1 tsp) vanilla essence
500 ml (2 cups) white cake flour
30 ml (2 Tbsp) baking powder
2,5 ml (½ tsp) salt
75 ml (5 Tbsp) cocoa powder

1. Preheat the oven to 180 °C. Grease or spray two standard cake tins, one large tin or a ring tin.
2. In a large mixing bowl, beat together the sugar, oil, water, egg yolks and vanilla essence for 2–3 minutes until thick.
3. Sift the flour, baking powder, salt and cocoa together in a separate bowl.
4. Sift the already sifted dry ingredients into the egg and sugar mixture and fold in lightly using a large metal spoon.
5. In a clean bowl, beat the egg whites to a soft peak (don't beat too hard as the egg whites dry out and become difficult to fold in). Fold into the cake batter lightly, using a large metal spoon.
6. Pour the cake batter into the prepared tins and bake for 40–45 minutes (depending on the tin used) or until well risen and springy to the touch, and the cake is pulling away slightly from the sides of the tin. Do not open the oven door until the cake looks and smells ready and at least 35 minutes are up.
7. Allow to cool for a few minutes before removing from the tin. Turn out onto a cooling rack and allow to cool completely before icing.

Tip: This cake improves with keeping and is even better on days two and three, if it lasts that long.

CHOCOLATE CAKE USING MILK CHOCOLATE

A few years ago I bought a chocolate cake at a school fundraiser. After tasting it, I hunted down the baker and asked her for the recipe. The secret is twofold: 100 g Cadbury milk chocolate and beating the eggs and sugar for 10 minutes in total. Thank you, Wendy!

Serves 12

250 ml (1 cup) boiling water
100 g Cadbury Dairy Milk chocolate
125 ml (½ cup) cocoa powder
250 ml (1 cup) canola oil
4 extra-large eggs
440 ml (1¾ cups) castor sugar
250 g cake flour (for accuracy use a scale to measure the flour)
15 ml (3 rounded teaspoons) baking powder
5 ml (1 tsp) vanilla essence
pinch of salt

1. Preheat the oven to 180 °C. Grease or spray two large cake tins.
2. Place the boiling water in a measuring jug, break up and add the chocolate and let it melt. Add the cocoa and oil.
3. In the bowl of an electric mixer, beat the eggs at high speed for 5 minutes.
4. Add the castor sugar and beat at high speed for another 5 minutes.
5. Add the water and chocolate mixture and beat at high speed for 1 minute.
6. Add the flour, baking powder, vanilla essence and salt and beat at high speed for 2 minutes.
7. Pour into the prepared cake tins and bake for 35 minutes until well risen and starting to pull away from the sides of the tins.
8. Allow to cool slightly in the tins, then turn out gently onto a cooling rack to cool completely.
9. Ice with the Butter Icing on page 200.

CARROT CAKE

This unbeatable carrot cake is a South African classic and appears in a number of local cookbooks. Both light and moist, it improves with keeping. I have changed the icing method to make it foolproof. Spooned into individual muffin cases (48), it makes delicious carrot muffins (bake for 30 minutes).

Serves 12–16

625 ml (2½ cups) cake flour
10 ml (2 tsp) baking powder
7,5 ml (1½ tsp) bicarbonate of soda
15 ml (1 Tbsp) mixed spice or speculaas spice
5 ml (1 tsp) salt
375 ml (1½ cups) light brown sugar
310 ml (1¼ cups) canola oil
4 extra-large eggs
500 ml (2 cups) grated carrots (2–3 large carrots)
250 ml (1 cup) tinned crushed pineapple
125 ml (½ cup) chopped pecan nuts or walnuts
60 ml (¼ cup) apricot jam or tart marmalade

CREAM CHEESE ICING
100 g butter
5 ml (1 tsp) vanilla essence
5 *x* 250 ml (5 cups) icing sugar
15–30 ml (1–2 Tbsp) boiling water
190 g cream cheese

1. Preheat the oven to 190 °C.
2. Sift together the flour, baking powder, bicarbonate of soda, spice and salt.
3. In another large bowl, beat together the sugar, oil and eggs until thick and light.
4. Add the carrots to the egg mixture, along with the drained crushed pineapple, nuts and jam and mix in thoroughly.
5. Sift in the dry ingredients and fold in gently.
6. Bake for 50–55 minutes in a well greased deep ring tin or in one large 28-cm loose-bottomed tin.
7. Remove from the oven and allow to cool before turning out.
8. Ice with cream cheese icing or simply dust with icing sugar.
9. To make the icing, melt the butter in a mixing bowl in the microwave oven.
10. Add the vanilla essence and icing sugar. Beat together very well with a wire whisk until smooth.
11. Add a tablespoon or two of boiling water to help mix to a stiff butter cream.
12. Add the cream cheese and mix in gently.

ANGEL CAKE

Serves 10

My family's favourite birthday cake, this American classic is light, airy and celebratory.

8 extra-large egg whites, at room temperature (use the yolks for crème brûlée and Béarnaise sauce)
8,5 ml (1¼ tsp) cream of tartar
pinch of salt
375 ml (1½ cups) white sugar
250 ml (1 cup) cake flour
5 ml (1 tsp) vanilla essence
5 ml (1 tsp) almond essence
icing sugar, for dusting

1. Preheat the oven to 180 °C. Spray (do not grease or butter) a ring tin or standard cake tin. I use a lovely heart-shaped silicone baking mould given to me by a Norwegian friend.
2. In a large mixing bowl, whisk the egg whites with the cream of tartar and salt until soft peaks form.
3. Gradually add 250 ml (1 cup) of the sugar, a tablespoon at a time, beating well in between additions until stiff peaks form.
4. Sift together the remaining 125 ml (½ cup) of sugar and the flour. Gently and gradually fold the flour and sugar mixture into the egg whites, being careful to keep it light and not release air. Fold in the vanilla and almond essence.
5. Spoon the mixture carefully into the prepared cake tin. Bake for 35–40 minutes until golden brown. Remove from the oven and cool for an hour before removing from the tin.
6. Serve dusted with icing sugar.

LEMON POLENTA CAKE

This wheat-free cake, adapted from the *River Cafe Cookbook*, can be served as a cake or a luscious dessert with mascarpone and berries.

Serves 8

250 g (1 cup) butter, at room temperature
250 g castor sugar
200 g (2 cups) ground almonds
5 ml (1 tsp) vanilla essence
3 extra-large eggs
grated rind and juice of 1 lemon
100 g polenta
5 ml (1 tsp) baking powder
pinch of salt

1. Preheat the oven to 170 °C. Grease or spray a standard cake tin.
2. Beat the butter and castor sugar together until pale and fluffy.
3. Mix in the almonds and vanilla essence. Add the eggs, one at a time, mixing after each addition.
4. Fold in the grated rind, lemon juice, polenta, baking powder and salt using a large metal spoon.
5. Spoon the mixture into the prepared tin and bake for 1 hour until set. Allow to cool down in the tin.
6. Serve at room temperature.

ORANGE SYRUP CAKE

(taken from *Cook with Ina Paarman*)

Serves 12

500 g (2 cups) butter, at room temperature
400 g (2 cups) sugar
5 extra-large eggs
10 ml (2 tsp) grated orange rind
450 g cake flour
15 ml (1 Tbsp) baking powder
2,5 ml (½ tsp) salt
5 ml (1 tsp) vanilla essence
190 ml (¾ cup) milk

Orange syrup
125 ml (½ cup) freshly squeezed orange juice
125 ml (½ cup) sugar
100 g butter
grated orange rind

1. Preheat the oven to 180 °C. Grease and flour a standard cake tin.
2. Cream the butter and sugar together with an electric beater until pale and fluffy.
3. Add the eggs, one by one, beating well after each one. Add the grated orange rind.
4. Sift the dry ingredients twice. Add the vanilla essence to the milk.
5. Alternately fold the dry ingredients and the milk into the creamed mixture. Do not stir too much but make sure the batter is blended.
6. Pour the batter into the prepared cake tin.
7. Bake for 1 hour until the cake is firm to the touch and a needle comes out clean. Cool for 10 minutes in the tin. Turn the cake out onto a cooling rack placed over a large plate.
8. Mix all the ingredients for the syrup in a bowl and microwave or heat in a saucepan until boiling and the sugar has dissolved.
9. Pour the hot syrup over the cake. Any syrup that drips onto the plate can be drizzled over again.

MUM'S BASIC VANILLA SPONGE CAKE

(coffee, chocolate or lemon)

Serves 8

Note: This recipe can be doubled for a larger cake.

125 ml (½ cup) canola oil
125 ml (½ cup) water
190 ml (¾ cup) sugar
5 ml (1 tsp) vanilla essence
3 extra-large eggs, separated
375 ml (1½ cups) cake flour
15 ml (1 Tbsp) baking powder
2,5 ml (½ tsp) salt

Butter Icing

125 ml (½ cup) melted butter
625 ml (2½ cups) icing sugar
5 ml (1 tsp) vanilla essence
30 ml (2 Tbsp) warm water

1. Preheat the oven to 180 °C. Grease and flour a loaf tin, two small round cake tins or a small ring tin.
2. In a bowl, beat together the oil, water, sugar, vanilla essence and egg yolks for 2 minutes.
3. Sift in the flour, baking powder and salt and fold in with a metal spoon.
4. In a separate bowl, beat the egg whites to a soft peak. Fold into the flour mixture.
5. Bake for 25–30 minutes. The cake should be well risen, firm to the touch and pulling away slightly from the sides of the tin.
6. Allow to stand for 5 minutes before turning out onto a cooling rack.
7. Cool completely before icing.
8. To make the icing, use a wire whisk to mix all the ingredients together to a thick, smooth paste. Ice the cake.

Variations:

~ **Chocolate cake:** Use 310 ml (1¼ cups) cake flour and 60 ml (¼ cup) cocoa powder, and add 30 ml (2 Tbsp) cocoa powder to the icing.

~ **Coffee cake:** Add 15 ml (1 Tbsp) instant coffee to the water for the cake mixture, and 10 ml (2 tsp) instant coffee to the water for the icing.

~ **Lemon cake:** Add 10 ml (2 tsp) grated lemon rind to the cake batter and the icing and substitute lemon juice for water in the icing.

FAVOURITE CUPCAKES

I just love this recipe for cupcakes. Iced with glacé icing, they make a magical old-fashioned teatime treat.

Makes 18 cupcakes

250 g (1 cup) butter, at room temperature
250 g icing sugar
4 extra-large eggs
250 g self-raising flour
125 ml milk
5 ml (1 tsp) vanilla essence

GLACÉ ICING
100 g sifted icing sugar
15 ml (1 Tbsp) boiling water
colourants of choice
sprinkles, for decorating

1. Preheat the oven to 180 °C. Line a cupcake tin with paper baking cups.
2. Beat the butter and icing sugar well until light and fluffy.
3. Add the eggs, one at a time, beating after each addition.
4. Add the flour, milk and vanilla essence and beat in well.
5. Spoon the mixture into the paper baking cups and bake for 20 minutes until well risen and golden brown.
6. Allow to cool completely on a cooling rack before icing.
7. Ice with glacé icing when completely cool. Decorate with sprinkles.
8. To make the icing, use a wire whisk to mix the icing sugar and boiling water together. Mix to a smooth and slightly runny cream. Add colourant of choice.
9. Ice the cupcakes immediately. Using a teaspoon, place a dollop of icing on each cupcake and allow the icing to form its own shape on the cupcake. Scatter sprinkles over immediately before the icing hardens, otherwise they won't stick.

APPLE CRUMBLE

My grandmother, who lived through two world wars, had great respect for tinned food. She only ever used unsweetened tinned apples in her apple crumble and she had a point. The apples are steamed in their own juice in the tins, cost very little, are convenient and easy to use and I challenge anyone to taste the difference once the crumble is cooked. Sunday lunch often ended with Goggomum's apple crumble with farm cream, and I have not tasted a better one.

Serves 4–6

2 standard tins (385 g each) or 1 large tin (765 g) apples (unsweetened)
5 ml (1 tsp) ground mixed spice
juice of 1 lemon
30 ml (2 Tbsp) sugar
190 ml (¾ cup) cake flour
60 ml (¼ cup) castor sugar
100 g butter
cream or ice cream, to serve

1. Preheat the oven to 180 °C.
2. Mix the apples, mixed spice, lemon juice and sugar together in a bowl and then pour into an ovenproof dish. The apples should be tightly packed and reach almost to the top of the dish, leaving a little room for the crumble.
3. In a bowl, rub the flour, castor sugar and butter together until the mixture resembles breadcrumbs. Scatter the mixture on top of the apples, covering them, and pat down lightly with your hand.
4. Bake for about 45 minutes until the crumble has browned and the apples are bubbling out slightly on the sides.
5. Serve hot or cold with cream or ice cream. It can be frozen for up to three weeks.

BAKED CHEESECAKE

This is a rich cheesecake, so keep the slices thin and serve with berries or other fruit to offset the richness.

Serves 10–12

1 packet (200 g) Tennis biscuits, finely crushed
100 g butter, melted
4 tubs (250 g each) plain smooth cream cheese
15 ml (1 Tbsp) custard powder
5 ml (1 tsp) vanilla essence
5 extra-large eggs
250 ml (1 cup) white sugar
250 ml (1 cup) sour cream
juice and grated rind of 1 lemon

1. Preheat the oven to 180 °C. Spray or grease a large springform cake tin.
2. Mix the biscuit crumbs and butter together and press down into the cake tin to form a base for the cheesecake.
3. In a large bowl and using a wire whisk, mix all the remaining ingredients together very well.
4. Pour carefully into the tin over the biscuit base.
5. Bake for 45 minutes until set and just starting to brown around the edges.
6. Switch off the oven and allow the cheesecake to cool in the oven.
7. Serve chilled or at room temperature.

CHOCOLATE TART

This rich, dark chocolate tart uses the shortcrust pastry on page 210.

Makes 2 standard tarts or 1 large tart

1 quantity Sweet Shortcrust Pastry (see page 210, adding 30 ml [2 Tbsp] castor sugar to the butter mixture)
300 g dark chocolate, broken up
200 g butter, cubed
3 extra-large eggs
60 g castor sugar

1. Preheat the oven to 180 °C.
2. Roll out the pastry and line two standard or one large loose-bottomed tart tin. Prick the pastry and allow to rest in the fridge for 15 minutes.
3. Bake the pastry blind (covered with uncooked beans or glass marbles) for 20 minutes.
4. While the pastry is baking, make the filling.
5. Melt the chocolate and butter together over very low heat, stirring slowly all the time. Do not allow to overheat. As soon as both the chocolate and butter have melted, remove from the heat.
6. Whisk in the eggs and castor sugar with a wire whisk.
7. When the pastry is cooked, remove from the oven and turn the heat down to 170 °C.
8. Allow the pastry to cool a little and then fill with the chocolate mixture.
9. Bake the tart(s) for 15 minutes until slightly set. Remove from the oven and cool completely before serving.

SHORTCRUST PASTRY

This pastry requires a food processor. Since my beloved friend and the best cook I know, Agnes de Vos, taught me this pastry, I have used no other.

This quantity covers 2 small tart tins or 1 large one

120 g cold butter, cubed
1 extra-large egg yolk
2,5 ml (½ tsp) salt
60 ml (¼ cup) cold water
375 ml (1½ cups) cake flour

1. Place all the ingredients, except the flour, in the bowl of the food processor. Pulse to combine and then blend for a couple of seconds until the mixture forms a porridge consistency.
2. Add the flour. Pulse 5–6 times and then blend until the dough comes together but is not smooth.
3. Place in a plastic bag and shape with your hands to a form a ball. Allow to rest in the fridge, covered, until it is needed.

Tip: If making a sweet pastry, add 30 ml (2 Tbsp) castor sugar to the butter mixture.

LEMON MERINGUE PIE

I find most lemon meringue pies to be rather sickly and insipid with hardly a hint of lemon. This one has a real lemon kick with a lovely smooth curd. It is rich, though, and not for the fainthearted.

Serves 6–8

1 packet (200 g) Tennis biscuits
125 ml (½ cup) melted butter
grated rind and juice of 4 lemons
1 tin (385 g) condensed milk
3 extra-large eggs, separated
2,5 ml (½ tsp) cream of tartar
180 g castor sugar
2,5 ml (½ tsp) baking powder

1. Preheat the oven to 180 °C.
2. Crush the biscuits. I do this by bashing the biscuits into crumbs using a double plastic shopping bag, tied loosely, and a rolling pin.
3. In a small bowl, mix the biscuit crumbs with the melted butter. Press the mixture into a shallow pie plate. Smooth with the back of a spoon.
4. In a bowl, mix together the lemon rind, lemon juice, condensed milk and egg yolks. Pour into the crumb base.
5. In a clean dry bowl, beat the egg whites to a soft peak. Add the cream of tartar and beat until the peaks are very stiff. Add the castor sugar, one tablespoon at a time, beating after each addition. Beat in the baking powder once the egg whites and sugar have formed a stiff meringue.
6. Spoon the meringue onto the egg mixture and cover gently. Swirl the meringue into peaks with the back of the spoon.
7. Bake for 20 minutes. Turn the oven off but leave the pie in the oven to cool down completely. This dries the meringue slightly.
8. Best served chilled.

Send them back
HAPPY!
I'm
Busy
Kellogg's
PEP

MILK TART

As a young bride and dairy farmer's wife, my mother had access to an abundance of milk. What better way of using it up than making milk tarts? The recipe below was and is widely used in farming communities. It is still served to overnight guests staying at the quintessential Karoo farm Wellwood outside Graaff-Reinet. Marion Rubidge will not only serve you a splendid home-cooked meal, she will also take you on a tour of the biggest Dicynodont (small to large herbivorous animals) collection in the world, housed in one of the old farm sheds.

It may not be the classic correct milk tart, but it is certainly my favourite. Perhaps because, more than anything else, it reminds me of the exceptional person that was my mum.

Serves 12

BASE
125 g butter, at room temperature
125 ml (½ cup) sugar
1 extra-large egg
500 ml (2 cups) cake flour
10 ml (2 tsp) baking powder
pinch of salt

FILLING
1 litre (4 cups) full-cream milk
15 ml (1 Tbsp) butter
37,5 ml (2½ Tbsp) cake flour
250 ml (1 cup) sugar
5 ml (1 tsp) vanilla essence
5 ml (1 tsp) almond essence (this is an important ingredient as it makes this milk tart stand out from others)
37,5 ml (2½ Tbsp) cornflour
2 extra-large eggs
cinnamon or mixed spice, for sprinkling

1. Preheat the oven to 180 °C. Spray two standard tart tins.
2. To make the base, cream the butter and sugar together.
3. Add the egg, flour, baking powder and salt and mix well.
4. Press into an even layer in the tart tins, prick with a fork, and bake for 10 minutes.
5. While the base is baking, prepare the filling.
6. In a large saucepan, heat the milk and butter to boiling point. Just before it boils, remove from the heat.
7. In a small bowl, mix all the remaining ingredients, except the cinnamon, using a wire whisk to form a smooth paste. Add to the hot milk and return to the heat, stirring gently until thick. Do not allow the filling to boil or burn. At boiling point, remove from the heat.
8. Pour the milk custard into the baked pastry. Sprinkle generously with cinnamon or mixed spice and allow to cool and set.
9. Serve slightly chilled.

CHOCOLATE ROULADE

Serves 8

180 g dark chocolate
5 extra-large eggs, separated
200 g castor sugar

FILLING
250 ml (1 cup) cream, whipped

1. Preheat the oven to 180 °C. Line a standard baking tray with baking paper. Make sure the baking paper is slightly bigger than the tray. Grease or spray the paper.
2. Melt the chocolate very gently in a glass bowl suspended over boiling water, or on medium in the microwave oven. Do not allow to overheat.
3. Beat the egg yolks and castor sugar together well.
4. Add the melted chocolate and stir in.
5. Whisk the egg whites to a firm peak (not stiff). Loosen the chocolate mixture with one spoonful of beaten egg white and then fold in the rest gently but thoroughly.
6. Pour the batter into the prepared baking tray, spreading it evenly.
7. Bake immediately for 20–25 minutes.
8. Take the roulade out of the oven and allow to cool completely.
9. Run a teatowel under the tap and then wring out well. Lightly cover the roulade with the damp towel.
10. Allow to stand for an hour or two (or overnight) before rolling up.
11. Fill with whipped cream and roll up.
12. Serve in slices with seasonal berries.

SWISS ROLL

Makes 8–10 slices

The key to a light Swiss roll is to beat the egg and sugar mixture for 10 minutes until really thick and pale.

4 extra-large eggs, separated
250 ml (1 cup) castor sugar
5 ml (1 tsp) vanilla essence
60 ml (¼ cup) milk
250 ml (1 cup) white cake flour
10 ml (2 tsp) baking powder
pinch of salt
125 ml (½ cup) strawberry or raspberry jam
extra castor sugar, for dusting

1. Preheat the oven to 180 °C. Line a standard baking tray with baking (not wax) paper, using canola or sunflower oil to make the paper stick to the tray. Brush the paper with the oil and then dust well with flour and a little castor sugar.
2. In a large bowl, beat the egg yolks and castor sugar for 10 minutes until stiff and pale.
3. Fold in the vanilla essence and milk.
4. Sift and fold in the flour, baking powder and salt, a little at a time, folding in carefully and thoroughly with each addition.
5. Pour the mixture into the prepared tray, ensuring that the mixture is evenly spread. Do this as gently as possible.
6. Bake for 10–12 minutes until firm to the touch and golden brown.
7. Soften the jam with a fork in a small bowl so that it is easy to spread when the cake comes out of the oven. Spread a damp teatowel on a flat surface and dust lightly with castor sugar.
8. Turn the cake onto the damp teatowel.
9. Allow to cool slightly (not too long or it will become difficult to roll) and then spread evenly with the jam.
10. Cut a shallow incision about 5 cm from one of the ends. This helps with the rolling. Roll carefully from that side and leave to cool on the seam.
11. Trim the ends with a sharp knife to neaten.

GINGER BISCUITS

In our house, ginger biscuits are eaten as fast as they are made. They are also a particular favourite of my mother-in-law, Joy. The recipe was sent to me by Margot Naude. The recipe yields about 150 biscuits. I have halved the quantities and achieved the same results.

Makes 72 biscuits

1 kg brown or white sugar
500 g (2 cups) butter, at room temperature
2 extra-large eggs
300 ml golden syrup
1 kg cake flour
75 ml (5 Tbsp) ground ginger
25 ml (5 tsp) bicarbonate of soda
25 ml (5 tsp) cream of tartar
5 ml (1 tsp) salt

1. Preheat the oven to 200 °C. Grease two very large baking trays or as many as you have.
2. In a bowl, mix together all the ingredients very well to form a thick dough. It is easiest in a mixer, using the biscuit attachment.
3. Roll into walnut-size balls and space well on the baking trays. Do this in batches.
4. Bake the biscuits for 10 minutes until golden brown. They should have small 'cracks' on the upper surface.
5. Cool on a cooling rack and store in an airtight container.

CHOCOLATE BROWNIES

Makes 16 squares

250 g (1 cup) butter
200 g dark chocolate (Woolworths Organic Dark Chocolate is excellent)
80 g cocoa powder
70 g (½ cup) cake flour
5 ml (1 tsp) baking powder
350 g castor sugar
50 g (½ cup) chopped walnuts (optional)
4 extra-large eggs

1. Preheat the oven to 180 °C. Spray or grease a square baking tin.
2. Melt the butter and chocolate together in a bowl in the microwave oven on medium setting, checking every 30 seconds that it has not overheated.
3. Using a wire whisk, add the cocoa powder, cake flour, baking powder, castor sugar and walnuts if using them. Whisk to a smooth consistency.
4. Beat in the eggs, one at a time.
5. Pour the mixture into the prepared baking tin and bake for 35 minutes.
6. Allow to cool before cutting into squares.

CHOCOLATE CRUNCHIES

Makes 32

My friend Sandy's mother made these to serve out of tins and Tupperware at school rugby matches. They are foolproof and travel well. The smooth cocoa icing and oat biscuit base make the perfect spectator treat. Be sure to make plenty as they disappear fast.

BASE

500 ml (2 cups) cake flour
500 ml (2 cups) oats
500 ml (2 cups) desiccated coconut
30 ml (2 Tbsp) cocoa powder
10 ml (2 tsp) baking powder
250 ml (1 cup) sugar
350 g butter, just melted

ICING

15 ml (1 Tbsp) cocoa powder
500 ml (2 cups) icing sugar
10 ml (2 tsp) butter
15 ml (1 Tbsp) hot water

1. Preheat the oven to 180 °C.
2. To make the base, mix all the ingredients together in a bowl.
3. Press the mixture down into a greased or sprayed baking tray and smooth the surface.
4. Bake for about 20 minutes until starting to brown at the edges and firm up.
5. Ice while still hot.
6. Place all the icing ingredients in a small saucepan and melt into a thick cream over low heat, stirring with a wire whisk or wooden spoon.
7. Pour the icing over the baked biscuit base, spreading it evenly. Allow to cool.
8. When cool and the icing has set, cut into squares.

OPEN

FUDGE

Makes 40 squares

This is the only fudge I like. Dark, with the proper fudge texture, the unbeatable flavour makes all the stirring worthwhile.

500 g castor sugar
80 ml (⅓ cup) water
125 g (½ cup) butter
30 ml (2 Tbsp) golden syrup
1 tin (385 g) condensed milk
5 ml (1 tsp) vanilla essence

1. In a heavy-bottomed saucepan, melt the castor sugar, water, butter and golden syrup together.
2. Bring to the boil, turn the heat down so that the mixture simmers and allow to cook, stirring occasionally, for 10 minutes until golden.
3. Remove from the heat and add the condensed milk, stirring all the time. Return to the heat and bring slowly back to a simmer. Stir all the time. Be careful – the mixture is very hot and very sticky and can cause terrible burns. Keep children away.
4. After 20–25 minutes the fudge should start turning a deeper brown colour and will start to fudge on the side of the pot. Watch carefully.
5. When it looks ready, drop a teaspoonful into a glass of cold water. Roll it into a little ball. The ball should not have a toffee texture. It isn't ready if it is still at that stage. The texture should be slightly grainy and set without being brittle. It takes about 45 minutes in total to reach this stage.
6. Add the vanilla essence, which will bubble up, and stir very well a few last times.
7. Pour into a small greased baking tray. Once the fudge has just set (it takes 10–15 minutes), cut into squares.
8. Cool completely and store in an airtight container.

Tip: Add drained and chopped preserved ginger to the fudge when adding the vanilla essence. The fudge will have lovely glistening pieces of shiny preserved ginger set into the squares, beautifully countering the sugar of the fudge.

Droste

ROCKY ROAD

Makes 40 squares

100 g butter
500 g chocolate (dark or milk or a combination)
30 ml (2 Tbsp) golden syrup
1 packet (200 g) shortbread biscuits, e.g. Eet-sum-mor
pinch of salt
100 g (1 cup) hazelnuts, walnuts, slivered almonds or pecan nuts
100 g marshmallows, snipped with scissors into quarters
100 g raisins or cranberries (optional)
100 g Rice Krispies® or Cornflakes

1. Grease and line a 23-cm square cake tin.
2. Melt the chocolate and syrup together in a small saucepan.
3. Mix in all the remaining ingredients.
4. Spoon into the prepared tin. Smooth gently with the back of a spoon but not too much. It should have a rough texture.
5. Allow to cool and set in the fridge for a couple of hours.
6. Turn out onto a dry surface and cut into squares. They are best served at room temperature and within a day or two of making them.
7. Store refrigerated in an airtight container for up to a week.

DATE SQUARES

Makes 56 generous or 64 standard squares

Probably my favourite lunchbox treat made by my beloved friend and almost-sister Jacqueline, these date squares are the perfect balance between healthy and indulgent. Easy to make and to transport, they last for a long time (four weeks) if kept in an airtight container.

PASTRY CRUMBLE

625 ml (2½ cups) white cake flour
625 ml (2½ cups) oats
250 ml (1 cup) white or brown sugar
2,5 ml (½ tsp) salt
300 g butter
5 ml (1 tsp) bicarbonate of soda dissolved in a little cold water
45 ml (3 Tbsp) water

FILLING

750 g dates, pitted and chopped
100 g currants
250 ml (1 cup) white or brown sugar
juice and grated rind of ½ lemon
250 ml (1 cup) water

1. In a large mixing bowl or in the bowl of a food processor, mix together the flour, oats, sugar and salt.
2. Cut the butter into cubes and rub it in with your fingers, or pulse together in the food processor.
3. Add the bicarbonate of soda and water and mix to form a dough.
4. Split the dough into two large balls and chill in the fridge for 30 minutes.
5. Place all the filling ingredients together in a lidded saucepan and heat through gently to soften and combine the ingredients. Simmer very gently for 5–10 minutes.
6. Leave to cool for 20 minutes.
7. Preheat the oven to 180 °C. Grease or spray a standard roasting pan (not a baking tray).
8. Place half the chilled pastry in the roasting pan and flatten with the back of a spoon to form the base.
9. Fill with the date mixture.
10. Crumble or grate the remaining pastry over the date mixture and press down gently.
11. Bake for 30 minutes until the pastry topping is firm and golden brown.
12. Cut into squares while still warm and allow to cool a bit in the roasting pan.
13. Cool completely on cooling racks.
14. Store in an airtight container. While these are best served fresh or within two weeks, they will last for up to a month.

MERINGUES

Makes 16 small or 9 large meringues

3 extra-large egg whites (use the yolks for crème brûlée or Béarnaise sauce)
pinch of cream of tartar
250 ml (1 cup) castor sugar
food colouring (optional)

1. Preheat the oven to 100 °C. Spray a large baking tray with nonstick cooking spray.
2. In a large dry bowl, beat together the egg whites and cream of tartar to a soft peak.
3. Add 15 ml (1 Tbsp) of castor sugar and beat well until it reaches a stiff peak.
4. Continue adding the castor sugar, a tablespoon at a time, beating well after each addition.
5. If you would like swirly coloured meringues (pink is my favourite as it makes the meringues look like large old-fashioned roses or camellias), add a couple of drops of colouring at this stage. Mix in gently but not thoroughly so that the swirls and marbling show up clearly on the finished meringue.
6. Spoon the meringue mixture onto the prepared baking tray.
7. Leave to bake for 3 hours.
8. Allow to cool completely before storing in an airtight container.

ICED PROFITEROLES

Makes 30

225 ml water
90 g butter
100 g white cake flour
pinch of salt
3 extra-large eggs

FILLING
250 ml (1 cup) fresh cream
5 ml (1 tsp) vanilla essence

ICING
Glacé Icing (see page 202) with 10 ml (2 tsp) cocoa powder added to the icing sugar

1. Preheat the oven to 200 °C. Grease or spray two baking trays.
2. Heat the water and butter together in a small saucepan until the butter has melted. Bring to the boil.
3. As soon as the mixture is boiling, add the flour and salt.
4. Keep the mixture over a medium heat for another 2 minutes, stirring all the time with a wooden spoon. Allow to cool.
5. Add the eggs, one at a time, beating well after each addition.
6. Place small teaspoonfuls of the mixture onto the baking trays, spaced well apart.
7. Bake for 10 minutes.
8. Turn up the oven to 220 °C and bake for another 20 minutes until well risen, golden brown and firm to the touch. Allow to cool completely before filling. Pierce each profiterole with a knitting needle or sharp knife to release any steam, which can make them soggy.
9. Beat the cream to a soft peak. Fold in the vanilla essence. Slice the profiteroles across the middle, but not right through. If the profiteroles still have a doughy centre, gently remove the bits of dough. Fill with cream.
10. Ice with Glacé Icing.

CHRISTA'S HEALTH SQUARES

When our daughter Sophia was born, my kind and lovely sister-in-law brought me these delicious health bars in hospital. They were the perfect counter to my physical depletion. They are also great for lunchboxes.

Makes 32

500 ml (2 cups) cake flour
500 ml (2 cups) desiccated coconut
750 ml (3 cups) oats
5 ml (1 tsp) salt
250 ml (1 cup) pecan nuts or walnuts
250 ml (1 cup) All-Bran® Flakes
250 ml (1 cup) raisins
250 ml (1 cup) brown sugar
2 extra-large eggs, lightly beaten
70 ml honey
250 g (1 cup) butter
10 ml (2 tsp) bicarbonate of soda

Optional
250 ml (1 cup) dried cranberries
125 ml (½ cup) sunflower and/or pumpkin seeds

1. Preheat the oven to 160 °C. Grease or spray a baking tray.
2. Mix together the flour, coconut, oats, salt, nuts, All-Bran Flakes, raisins and sugar in a large mixing bowl.
3. Add the beaten eggs and mix in.
4. Melt the honey and butter together and add the bicarbonate of soda. Allow to cool slightly. Mix into the fruit and egg mixture.
5. Press the mixture down lightly into the prepared baking tray.
6. Bake for 30–35 minutes.
7. Cut into squares while still warm and allow to cool in the pan.

Tip: If using the cranberries and seeds, add another egg and 30 ml (2 Tbsp) butter.

LEMON CURD SQUARES

For years a friend of mine, Cheryl, described to me the lemon cake her mother made and how she wished she could find the recipe. When I opened Christine Capendale's excellent *Baking for Pleasure & Profit*, I knew I had found it! I have adapted the method and cooking times slightly to give more of a lemon curd centre. Cheryl also suggested topping the lemon squares with flaked almonds as her mother used to. After trying this recipe a couple of times in a regular baking tray, I invested in a solid baking tray with raised sides. It has made all the difference.

Makes 24 squares

Base

250 g (1 cup) butter, at room temperature
190 ml (¾ cup) icing sugar
500 ml (2 cups) cake flour

Filling

6 extra-large eggs
500 ml (2 cups) castor sugar
juice of 3–4 lemons [you need 160 ml (⅔ cup); finely grate the rind before squeezing]
190 ml (¾ cup) cake flour
7,5 ml (1½ tsp) baking powder
1 packet (100 g) flaked almonds (optional)
icing sugar, for dusting

1. Preheat the oven to 180 °C. Spray or grease a baking tray with butter.
2. To make the base, cream the softened butter and icing sugar together and add the flour to make the dough, OR place all three ingredients in the bowl of a food processor and pulse to blend until just pulling together into a dough.
3. Press the dough into the greased tray and keep it in the fridge until the oven has reached the correct temperature.
4. Bake for 25 minutes until evenly golden brown.
5. Turn the oven down to 150 °C.
6. To make the filling, beat the eggs and castor sugar well but not until fluffy. If the eggs and castor sugar are beaten until fluffy, the cake is spongier and light. Up to you!
7. Add the lemon juice, lemon rind, flour and baking powder and mix until smooth (a wire whisk works well).
8. Pour the filling onto the baked crust, sprinkle over the flaked almonds if using them and bake at 150 °C for 40 minutes. The filling should be set and golden brown but it should still jiggle a little at the touch.
9. Allow to cool completely before cutting into squares.
10. Sift over icing sugar before serving.

SHORTBREAD

I long for homemade shortbread in a Cornishware biscuit barrel on the Welsh dresser in my grandparents' sitting room! It was resolutely there, along with the iced water in a flask and lemon cordial. The memory of the particular light thrown of an East Griqualand afternoon, and the comfort of the good people who raised me, makes everything possible.

Makes 32

700 g cake flour
500 g (2 cups) butter, at room temperature but not warm
200 g castor sugar, plus extra for sprinkling once baked
pinch of salt

1. Preheat the oven to 100 °C.
2. In a large mixing bowl, rub together all the ingredients until the mixture resembles breadcrumbs. Form into a loose dough.
3. Press the dough into a large baking tray and flatten, using your fingers, to about 2 cm thick.
4. Prick with a fork all over.
5. Bake for about 1 hour.
6. Remove from the oven and cut into fingers while still hot.
7. Sprinkle with castor sugar before serving.

would you

CHEESE BISCUITS

Once a year our friends Sarah and Pete host a drinks party in their lovely home. I always position myself next to the plate of star-shaped cheese biscuits. Easy to make and delicious, these cheese biscuits or straws (if that is how you choose to serve them) make a wonderful snack. Serve as soon as possible!

Makes 16 round biscuits

75 g butter
75 g flour
75 g mature Cheddar cheese, grated
2,5 ml (½ tsp) mustard powder
beaten egg or a little milk, for brushing
sesame seeds and/or poppy seeds, for sprinkling

1. Preheat the oven to 180 °C. Spray a baking tray with nonstick cooking spray.
2. Mix all the ingredients in the bowl of a food processor or rub together by hand.
3. Chill the dough in the fridge for 20 minutes.
4. Roll out to 5 mm on a lightly floured surface. Cut into straws or your chosen shapes. Twist the straws if preferred. Place on the prepared tray.
5. Brush with egg or milk and sprinkle with sesame seeds.
6. Bake for 10–12 minutes until golden brown.
7. Allow to cool and serve on the same day.

CHEESE TARTLETS

Makes 24 tartlets

1 quantity Shortcrust Pastry (see page 210)

FILLING

1 tub (250 g) plain smooth cream cheese
2 extra-large eggs
1 bunch spring onions or chives, finely chopped (optional)
5 ml (1 tsp) Dijon mustard
100 g (1 cup) Cheddar cheese, grated
50 g Parmesan cheese, grated
salt and pepper
½ red pepper, sliced

1. Preheat the oven to 200 °C.
2. Roll out the pastry, about 5 mm thick. Cut it into circles with a glass or pastry cutter to make 24 rounds. Prick the pastry rounds with a fork.
3. Place the pastry rounds in shallow muffin or cupcake tins. Bake for 10 minutes to partially cook the pastry (it shouldn't brown).
4. Mix all the filling ingredients, except the red pepper, together in a bowl.
5. Fill each pastry cup with a tablespoon of filling. Top with a slice of red pepper.
6. Place in the oven and bake for 10–12 minutes until puffed up and browned on top.
7. Serve hot.

SQUIDGIES

Makes 32 squares

This invaluable recipe was given to me by a family full of wonderful cooks who cater for all generations, all the time. Thank you Sue, Jenny, Adrianne and Sarah. These are great as teatime treats, for weekends away, hikes, lunchboxes and just about any time.

500 ml (2 cups) white cake flour
500 ml (2 cups) white or brown sugar
500 ml (2 cups) desiccated coconut
500 ml (2 cups) dried fruitcake mix
10 ml (2 tsp) baking powder
2 extra-large eggs
200 g butter, melted

1. Preheat the oven to 180 °C.
2. Mix all the ingredients together and press into a standard greased baking tray.
3. Bake for 30 minutes until firm and slightly risen.
4. Cool slightly and then cut into squares.
5. Store in an airtight container.

PUDDINGS

PEARS IN RED WINE

Serves 6

300 ml red wine
125 g sugar
1 whole piece of lemon rind
1 cinnamon stick
3 whole cloves
6 pears, peeled

1. In a medium saucepan (in which the pears should fit snugly), bring the wine, sugar, lemon rind, cinnamon and gloves to the boil and then turn down the heat to a simmer.
2. Simmer for 5 minutes until the sugar has melted and the mixture is starting to turn a little syrupy.
3. Add the pears, stalks up. If the bottoms of the pears are a little uneven, trim them with a paring knife so that they stand upright in the saucepan. The liquid should almost cover the pears.
4. Simmer for 20 minutes until the pears are cooked through and the sauce is syrupy. Allow to cool in the saucepan.
5. Serve hot or cold with fresh cream, ice cream, crème fraîche, mascarpone and, if you have the time, toasted flaked almonds.

CRÈME BRÛLÉE

It is not necessary to own a blow torch to make crème brûlée. The grill of an oven works just as well, with the advantage of being able to grill all your ramekins at the same time. Crème brûlée is essentially a cooked cream custard and really easy to make. You do need time to allow the custards to set and chill before and after grilling the sugar. To take the pressure off, make the custard pots the day before you need them and then grill the sugar an hour or so before you actually serve them.

Makes 10 standard ramekins

6 extra-large egg yolks (use the whites for Meringues on page 232 or the Angel Cake on page 194)
125 ml (½ cup) sugar
250 ml (1 cup) milk
500 ml (2 cups) fresh cream
5 ml (1 tsp) vanilla essence
60 ml (¼ cup) castor sugar, for topping

1. Preheat the oven to 150 °C. Spray 10 ramekin dishes with nonstick cooking spray.
2. Whisk the egg yolks and sugar together until thick and pale.
3. Gently whisk in the milk, cream and vanilla essence.
4. Fill the ramekins to just below the lip with the custard mixture.
5. Pour boiling water into a deep roasting pan or baking tray. Place the filled ramekins carefully into the water bath (*bain-marie*). The water should reach to just above halfway on the sides of the ramekins. Place the pan into the oven and bake for 1½ hours.
6. Remove from the oven and allow to cool out of the water bath. Once the custard pots are cool, cover each one with plastic wrap and chill in the fridge for at least 4 hours or overnight.
7. An hour or two before serving, preheat the oven grill to high. Place the set custard pots on a baking tray and sprinkle over the castor sugar, forming a thin film of sugar on each one. Place under the grill on the highest rack and keep a close eye on the ramekins. As soon as the sugar has melted and formed a caramel-coloured puddle on each ramekin, remove from the heat. Allow to cool down and then return to the fridge until ready to serve.

CHOCOLATE SELF-SAUCING PUDDING

My son, Tom, asked me to include this recipe as 'Sunday lunch isn't the same without chocolate pudding'. Immensely satisfying and made with standard kitchen ingredients, this chocolate pudding is the stuff of childhood dreams. It is made with cocoa and not chocolate, so isn't too rich or expensive. The sauce develops during the cooking process.

Serves 4–6

250 ml (1 cup) self-raising flour
30 ml (2 Tbsp) cocoa powder
125 ml (½ cup) brown sugar
80 g butter, melted
125 ml (½ cup) milk
1 extra-large egg

TOPPING/SAUCE
30 ml (2 Tbsp) cocoa powder
190 ml (¾ cup) brown sugar
310 ml (1¼ cups) boiling water

fresh cream, custard or ice cream, to serve

1. Preheat the oven to 180 °C. Spray a smallish 2-litre capacity ovenproof dish with nonstick cooking spray.
2. Sift the flour and cocoa together in a bowl. Add the sugar.
3. Mix the melted butter, milk and egg together with a fork in a small bowl or jug. Add to the flour mixture and beat with a wire whisk until smooth.
4. Pour the batter into the prepared baking dish and smooth gently.
5. For the topping, combine the cocoa and sugar and sprinkle over the top of the pudding mixture.
6. Carefully pour the boiling water over the cocoa and sugar, using the back of a large serving spoon to prevent splashing.
7. Bake for 40 minutes until risen and firm to the touch.
8. Serve with fresh cream, custard or ice cream.

MALVA PUDDING

Serves 8

250 ml (1 cup) castor sugar
2 extra-large eggs
15 ml (1 Tbsp) smooth apricot jam (if using homemade, strain so that it is smooth)
250 ml (1 cup) white cake flour
pinch of salt
5 ml (1 tsp) bicarbonate of soda
50 g butter, melted in 125 ml (½ cup) milk
5 ml (1 tsp) brown or white vinegar

SAUCE

250 ml (1 cup) fresh cream
60 ml (¼ cup) white or brown sugar
100 g butter
125 ml (½ cup) water
5 ml (1 tsp) vanilla essence

1. Preheat the oven to 180 °C.
2. Grease or spray an ovenproof baking dish.
3. In a large bowl, beat together the castor sugar and eggs until pale and fluffy, about 3 minutes.
4. Beat in the apricot jam.
5. Sieve together the flour, salt and bicarbonate of soda. Fold in gently.
6. Fold in the milk, butter and vinegar.
7. Pour the mixture into the prepared baking dish and smooth gently.
8. Bake in the preheated oven for 45 minutes.
9. While the pudding is baking, place all the sauce ingredients into a saucepan. Bring to a simmer to allow the butter to melt. Keep on the stove.
10. When the pudding is cooked through and light and springy to the touch, remove from the oven and pour over the warm sauce.
11. Serve warm with custard or ice cream.

BAKED ALMOND & LEMON PUDDING

Serves 6–8

150 g butter, at room temperature
310 ml (1¼ cups) castor sugar
5 extra-large eggs, separated
200 ml white cake flour
80 ml (⅓ cup) ground almonds
80 ml (⅓ cup) milk
100 ml freshly squeezed lemon juice (or juice of 3 large lemons)
15 ml (1 Tbsp) grated lemon rind

1. Preheat the oven to 180 °C.
2. Cream the butter and castor sugar together. Add the egg yolks, one at a time, beating well after each addition.
3. Sift in the flour and add the almonds, milk, lemon rind and lemon juice.
4. Whisk the egg whites to a soft peak, and gently fold into the mixture.
5. Spoon into a greased ovenproof dish or 6 individual ramekins and place in a roasting pan half-filled with boiling water. Bake for 40 minutes.
6. Serve immediately with cream, crème fraîche or vanilla ice cream. The pudding should have created its own sauce.

RIGHT: Traditional Christmas Pudding, recipe on page 262

TRADITIONAL CHRISTMAS PUDDING

I love Christmas pudding but I don't love the overly sweet, raisin-heavy version available commercially. This recipe is easy to make, has almost no flour and delivers a light and flavourful end to a Christmas meal. Serve with brandy butter.

The pudding mixture needs to stand overnight, so start the day before. It is important to have a heatproof mixing bowl (1,5 litres) with a lip or an old-fashioned pudding bowl to steam the pudding.

Serves 12

PUDDING
100 g butter (or suet if you can get it), at room temperature
50 g self-raising flour
100 g fresh breadcrumbs (make by whizzing bread in a food processor)
5 ml (1 tsp) ground mixed spice
pinch of nutmeg
pinch of ground cinnamon
250 g treacle sugar
100 g sultanas
100 g raisins
100 g currants
25 g mixed candied peel
100 g slivered almonds
1 Granny Smith apple, peeled, cored and grated
grated rind of 1 orange
grated rind of 1 lemon
2 extra-large eggs
75 ml (5 Tbsp) brandy
100 ml stout

BRANDY BUTTER
125 g (½ cup) butter, at room temperature
250 g icing sugar, sifted
45 ml (3 Tbsp) brandy

1. Mix together the butter, flour, breadcrumbs, spices, sugar, dried fruit, candied peel, almonds, grated apple and rinds in a bowl.
2. In a separate bowl, mix together the eggs, brandy and stout with a fork. Mix this into the fruit mixture, combining well.
3. Cover with plastic wrap and leave in a cool place or in the fridge overnight.
4. Preheat the oven to 140°C. Grease a lipped mixing bowl or a pudding basin. Boil the kettle.
5. Fill the prepared mixing bowl or pudding basin with the pudding mixture, smoothing the surface. Cover with a double layer of baking paper, tied with string. Make a handle with extra string so that it is easy to lift the pudding in and out of the boiling water.
6. Place the bowl or basin in a roasting pan and fill to at least halfway with the boiling water. Cover the roasting pan and pudding with a sheet of foil, tucking it in to stay in place.
7. Place the roasting pan and pudding in the oven and leave to steam for 5–6 hours. Check from time to time (not more than twice) that there is still sufficient water to steam the pudding. If necessary, top up with boiling water from the kettle.
8. Serve warm with brandy butter. If the pudding has cooled, warm through briefly in the microwave oven.
9. To make the brandy butter, beat all the ingredients together with a wire whisk or a hand beater.
10. Store, covered, in the fridge until needed. Reheat before serving.

PAVLOVA

Serves 8–10

4 extra-large egg whites (use the yolks for crème brûlée or Béarnaise sauce)
pinch of cream of tartar
pinch of salt
450 g castor sugar
20 ml (4 tsp) white grape vinegar
40 ml (8 tsp) cornflour
3 drops vanilla essence
cream or mascarpone and fruit, to fill

1. Preheat the oven to 180 °C. Spray a large baking tray with nonstick cooking spray.
2. In a large, dry mixing bowl, beat the egg whites to a soft peak with the cream of tartar and salt.
3. Beat the egg whites to a stiff peak, adding 15 ml (1 Tbsp) of castor sugar at a time, beating well after each addition. Keep beating until all the sugar has been added.
4. Lastly, beat in the vinegar, cornflour and vanilla essence.
5. Spoon the meringue mixture onto the prepared baking tray, shaping it into a large dish shape with slightly raised sides. Using the back of a spoon, drag up little peaks of the meringue around the side to give it an attractive look.
6. Bake for 20 minutes until just starting to brown in patches. Turn the oven down to 100 °C and bake for another 20 minutes. Turn the oven off and allow the meringue to cool in the oven.
7. Fill with whipped cream or mascarpone and any choice of fruits in season. Adding a teaspoon of vanilla essence and a tablespoon of castor sugar to the whipped cream turns it into a lovely vanilla cream.

FRUIT SALAD

Serves 4

BASIC MIXTURE

2 oranges, peeled, depipped and and cut into chunks
2 green or red apples, cored and cut into chunks
1 pear, cored and cut into chunks
1 banana, sliced
80 ml (⅓ cup) honey
juice of 1 lemon

SEASONAL FRUIT TO ADD

nectarines, peaches, plums, mangoes, pineapples, grapes, spanspek, watermelon, guavas, granadillas, pawpaw, berries, cherries

1. Cut up the fruit in the basic mixture and place in a bowl. Mix the honey and lemon juice together and pour over.
2. Into the basic mixture, add three or four seasonal fruits and mix in gently.
3. Store, covered, in the fridge.

MANGO & YOGHURT DESSERT

Serves 8

8 fresh mangoes, peeled and sliced
500 ml (2 cups) double-cream Greek yoghurt (if not available, use 250 ml [1 cup] plain low-fat yoghurt folded together with 250 ml [1 cup] whipped cream)
60 ml (¼ cup) treacle sugar

1. Place the mangoes in a glass serving dish.
2. Spoon over the yoghurt and smooth the surface.
3. Sprinkle evenly with the sugar and refrigerate for 3–4 hours. The sugar will melt and form a crunchy crust on top of the yoghurt.
4. Serve chilled.

CHOCOLATE MOUSSE

As a treat, our father would take us for dinner at the Anton van Wouw restaurant before going on to see a show at The Alhambra in Johannesburg. They served a chocolate mousse popular at the time, which went out of fashion and was replaced by creamier, fussier and sweeter chocolate concoctions which never really matched up to that utterly delicious one. Fairly recently, the owner of Hedge House guesthouse, Judy England, in Newlands, Cape Town, served it to me again. I almost cried with relief, joy and a nostalgic longing for those precious family outings.

Serves 8–10

4 extra-large eggs, separated
125 ml (½ cup) fresh cream
200 g dark chocolate
15 ml (1 Tbsp) butter

1. In a clean, dry bowl, whip the egg whites to soft peak stage. Do not overbeat as they will become dry.
2. Beat the cream to soft peak stage. Do not overbeat as it will become lumpy.
3. Melt the chocolate and butter together very slowly in a bowl in the microwave oven on medium. Do not overheat. Stir to a smooth paste with a wire whisk and add the egg yolks. Mix well.
4. Fold the cream into the chocolate mixture, followed by the egg whites.
5. Spoon into individual ramekins, glasses or a single attractive glass serving dish, and refrigerate overnight or for at least 8 hours until set.

EASY ICE CREAM

Serves 6–8

500 ml (2 cups) fresh cream
2 small tubs (175 ml each) plain yoghurt
1 tin (385 g) condensed milk
10 ml (2 tsp) vanilla essence

1. Beat the cream until stiff but not lumpy. It should still fall off the beaters gently.
2. Beat in the yoghurt, condensed milk and vanilla essence.
3. Pour into a container with a lid and freeze for 12 hours.

VANILLA POD ICE CREAM

Serves 12–14

6 extra-large eggs, separated
220 g castor sugar
10 ml (2 tsp) vanilla essence
1 vanilla pod or 1 tsp (5 ml) vanilla paste
1 litre (4 cups) fresh cream

1. Beat the egg yolks until pale. Gradually add the castor sugar (spoon by spoon with beaters running) until the mixture has doubled in volume and is pale.
2. Add the vanilla essence. Split the vanilla pod, scrape out the seeds and add the seeds to the mixture.
3. Beat the cream to soft peak stage and fold it into the egg mixture.
4. Beat the egg whites to soft peak stage and fold in.
5. Freeze in batches in an ice-cream machine, or overnight in the freezer.

QUICK & EASY CHRISTMAS ICE CREAM BOMBE

This is a useful alternative to traditional Christmas pudding. It also suits the South African December climate very well.

Serves 16

1 tub (2 litres) good quality vanilla ice cream, softened slightly
1 tub (2 litres) good quality chocolate ice cream, softened slightly
1 packet (100 g) slivered almonds, toasted (on a baking tray in the oven until nicely browned)
1 tin (420 g) black cherries, drained

1. Spray a large, attractively shaped mixing bowl with nonstick cooking spray.
2. In layers of your choice, layer the ice cream, nuts and cherries, alternating the layers of ice cream to achieve a marbled effect.
3. Cover and freeze.
4. When serving, run the bowl under lukewarm water, run a knife around the inside and turn out onto a large serving plate.
5. Pour over hot Bar One Chocolate Sauce (see page 276) and decorate with any fun Christmas decorations or fresh berries and cherries.
6. Eat quickly as the time of year and the hot chocolate sauce speed up the melting process.

THREE CHOCOLATE SAUCES

PANTRY CHOCOLATE SAUCE
Makes 1 generous cup

60 ml (¼ cup) cocoa powder
125 ml (½ cup) milk
250 ml (1 cup) brown sugar
5 ml (1 tsp) vanilla essence
30 ml (2 Tbsp) butter
pinch of salt

1. Place all the ingredients in a saucepan and slowly bring to the boil, stirring with a wire whisk.
2. Simmer gently for 5 minutes until the sauce has thickened.
3. Serve hot.
4. Store, covered, in the fridge. An old jam jar works well.

DARK CHOCOLATE SAUCE
Makes ½ cup

100 g dark chocolate, broken into pieces
15 ml (1 Tbsp) golden syrup
15 ml (1 Tbsp) butter

1. In a small glass bowl on medium heat in the microwave oven or a small saucepan over low heat on the stove, warm all the ingredients together very slowly, stirring regularly with a wire whisk until runny and smooth.
2. Serve hot.

BAR ONE CHOCOLATE SAUCE
Makes a scant 2 cups

250 ml (1 cup) fresh cream
8 giant Bar Ones (100 g each), chopped into chunks

1. In a medium-sized saucepan, heat the cream but do not boil. Remove from the heat.
2. Tip the chopped Bar Ones into the hot cream and stir with a wire whisk.
3. Place the saucepan back on very low heat and stir frequently until the chocolate and toffee have melted entirely.
4. Store in a covered plastic or ceramic jug in the fridge for two weeks.
5. Reheat in the microwave oven when serving.

CUSTARD

Instant vanilla custard powder is a useful pantry ingredient. Simply follow the cooking instructions for a perfectly acceptable and child-pleasing pouring or thick custard. However, if you are looking for something a little more delicate and authentic, this classic custard is a real treat. Served with fresh or stewed fruit, meringues, hot chocolate or malva pudding, it makes a comforting end to a meal.

Makes 1 generous cup

250 ml (1 cup) full-cream milk or cream or half and half (depending how rich you would like the custard)
2 egg yolks (the whites can be frozen and used for meringues)
5 ml (1 tsp) cornflour
5 ml (1 tsp) vanilla essence
pinch of vanilla powder or a squirt of vanilla paste
45 g castor sugar

1. In a small saucepan, bring the milk and/or cream to just below boiling point. Remove from the heat.
2. Beat the egg yolks, cornflour, vanilla essence and castor sugar in a glass bowl until thick and creamy.
3. Pour a bit of the scalded milk into the egg mixture and mix in to acclimatise the eggs, and then pour back into the saucepan.
4. Stir continuously with a wire whisk or a wooden spoon over a moderate heat until the mixture thickens. Remove at boiling point.
5. Serve hot or cold.
6. It will keep, covered, in the fridge for up to a week.

INDEX

A

almond & lemon pudding, baked 258
Angel cake 194
antipasto 44
apple crumble 204
apples and onions, slow-cooked pork neck on a bed of 150
aubergines 68, 82

B

bacon & mushroom risotto 74
baked
  almond & lemon pudding 258
  cheesecake 206
  jacket potatoes 92
  scones 36
  stuffed peppers 84
  sweet potato & pumpkin with cinnamon, brown sugar & orange 98
banana bread 180
basil pesto 160
beans, lemony mustard green 80
béarnaise sauce 136
beetroot & feta salad 104
biscuits, cheese 242
biscuits, ginger 220
bobotie 142
bolognaise-style mince for cottage pie & lasagne 138
bran muffins, 30-day 38
bread. *See also* loaf
  banana 180
  bruschetta DIY 44
  farm 176
  Lindsay's quick & easy seed loaf 178
breakfast porridges 22
bredie 144
broccoli & cauliflower cheese 96
brownies, chocolate 222
bruschetta DIY 44
bulgur wheat salad 64
buttermilk rusks 182
butternut & coriander couscous 66

C

cabbage salad 106
cake
  Angel 194
  carrot 192
  cheesecake, baked 206
  chocolate, using milk chocolate 190
  Diana's chocolate 188
  Gogo van der Riet's Christmas 186
  lemon polenta 196
  Mum's basic vanilla sponge 200
  orange syrup 198
cauliflower & broccoli cheese 96
cheese biscuits 242
cheese tartlets 244
cheesecake, baked 206
chicken
  & vegetables, roast 128
  chutney 124
  coq au vin 116
  curry 120
  liver pâté 164
  Marbella 126
  pie 122
  with lemon, olives & garlic, slow-roasted 118
chips 56
chocolate
  brownies 222
  cake, Diana's 188
  cake using milk chocolate 190

crunchies 224
mousse 270
chocolate
roulade 216
self-saucing pudding 254
tart 208
chocolate sauce
Bar One 276
dark 276
pantry 276
Christa's health squares 236
Christmas
cake, Gogo van der Riet's 186
ice cream bombe, quick and easy 274
pudding, traditional 262
coq au vin 116
cottage pie 138
couscous, butternut & coriander 66
crème brûlée 252
crumble, apple 204
crunchies, chocolate 224
cupcakes, favourite 202
curry, chicken 120
curry, lentil & vegetable 70
custard 278

D

date squares 230
dessert, mango & yoghurt 268
Diana's chocolate cake 188

E

eggs 15, 24, 26, 28, 30,

F

fillet with béarnaise sauce 136
fishcakes, tuna 62
French toast 24
fruit salad 266
fudge 226

G

gazpacho 50
ginger biscuits 220
Gogo van der Riet's Christmas cake 186
granola 18
green beans, lemony mustard 80
green salad & dressing 102
grilled mixed peppers 86

H

hamburgers & chips 56
health squares, Christa's 236
hummus 162

I

ice cream
bombe, quick and easy Christmas 274
easy 272
vanilla pod 273
iced profiteroles 234

K

kedgeree 28

L

lamb, slow-cooked 146
lasagne 138
lemon
& almond pudding, baked 258
curd squares 238
meringue pie 212
polenta cake 196
lemony mustard green beans 80
lentil & vegetable curry 70
Lindsay's quick & easy seed loaf 178
liver, chicken 164
loaf, Lindsay's quick & easy seed 178
loaves, pressed picnic 76

M
macaroni cheese 60
Maltabella (sorghum porridge) 22
malva pudding 256
mango & yoghurt dessert 268
mayonnaise, quick & easy 170
mealie meal porridge 22
meatballs 140
melanzane 82
meringue pie, lemon 212
meringues 232
milk tart 214
mince, bolognaise-style, for cottage pie & lasagne 138
mousse, chocolate 270
muffins, 30-day bran 38
Mum's basic vanilla sponge cake 200
mushroom & bacon risotto 74

O
oats porridge 22
omelette 26
onion soup 48
orange syrup cake 198
oxtail 132

P
paella 156
pancakes 32
pastry, shortcrust 210
pâté, chicken liver 164
pavlova 264
pears in red wine 250
peppers, baked stuffed 84
peppers, grilled mixed 86
pie, chicken 122
pie, lemon meringue 212
pizza 58
polenta cake, lemon 196
pork neck on a bed of apples & onions 150
porridge
  oats 22
  sorghum (Maltabella) 22
  white mealie meal 22
  yellow mealie meal 22
potato(es)
  bake 94
  baked jacket 92
  roast 88
  salad with mayonnaise 108
  salad with vinaigrette 110
  sweet 98
  wedges, roast, with rosemary 90
profiteroles, iced 234
pudding
  baked almond & lemon 258
  chocolate self-saucing 254
  malva 256
  traditional Christmas 262
pumpkin & baked sweet potato with cinnamon, brown sugar & orange 98

Q
quiche, tomato & pesto 54

R
ratatouille 68
risotto, bacon & mushroom 74
roast
  beef & Yorkshire pudding 134
  chicken and vegetables 128
  potatoes 88
  potato wedges with rosemary 90
rocky road 228
roulade, chocolate 216
rusks, buttermilk 182

S
salad
  beetroot & feta 104

bulgur wheat 64
cabbage 106
fruit 266
green, & dressing 102
potato salad with mayonnaise 108
potato salad with vinaigrette 110
sandwiches 76
sauces
Bar One chocolate 276
basic tomato 168
basil pesto 160
béarnaise 136
chocolate 276
chocolate self-saucing 254
cinnamon, brown sugar & orange 98
dark chocolate 276
gravy 134
hummus 162
orange syrup 198
pantry chocolate 276
pesto 54
quick & easy mayonnaise 170
salad dressing 102
tartare 166
vinaigrette 110
scones 36
seed loaf, Lindsay's quick & easy 178
shortbread 240
shortcrust pastry 210
sorghum porridge 22
soup, basic vegetable 46
soup, onion 48
sponge cake, Mum's basic vanilla 200
squidgies 246
stewed fruit 20
stuffed peppers, baked 84
sunflower seeds, toasted 98
sweetcorn fritters 30
sweet potato & pumpkin with cinnamon, brown sugar & orange, baked 98
Swiss roll 218

T
tart, chocolate 208
tart, milk 214
tartare sauce 166
tartlets, cheese 244
tomato & pesto quiche 54
tomato sauce, basic 168
traditional Christmas pudding 262
tuna fishcakes 62

V
vanilla pod ice cream 273
vegetable & lentil curry 70
vegetable soup, basic 46

W
waffles 34
wheat salad, bulgur 64

Y
yoghurt & mango dessert 268
Yorkshire pudding, roast beef & 134

ACKNOWLEDGEMENTS

This book was made possible by the brilliant and sensitive curatorship of editor Annake Müller, designer Marius Roux, food stylist Caro Alberts, Tani Kirsten who made the food and photographer Myburgh du Plessis. This talented team has turned *For Friends & Family* into the magnificent book that it is. Thank you.

Thank you to my sister Pippa Hetherington for her exquisite photos of family and friends and beautiful things. And for being the remarkable person she is.

Thank you to my mentor Eloise Wessels, and friend and publisher Marga Stoffer for believing in me. Thank you to a terrific sales and marketing team at NB Publishers, including Tracey-Lee Gerber, Petro du Toit, Eben Pienaar, Marietta Schoeman, Liza Daniels, Petra Maree, Clare Williams, Jean Pieters and Karen Dry.

Thank you to the following people for being my inspiration and for being (or having been) in the world:

Adrian Anderson, Agnes de Vos, Aubrey Stubbs, Audrey Brown, Bridget Lane, Candice Kerchhoff, Christa Buys, Daniela Massenz, Deb Naughton, Debbie Dickson, Diana Stubbs, Dirk de Vos, Elnor Leach, Gill Cullinan, Guy Stubbs, Hamsa Lilley, Helen and Ian Hetherington, Helen During, Herman van der Schijff, Hillary Keegin, Ingie Bryden, Jacqueline Lamprecht, Janice Probyn, Janine O'Connor, Jeremy Stubbs, Joan Stubbs, Johann van der Schijff, John Butler, Joy Mwela, Kendyl Carikas, Kimon Phitides, Lindsay Wentworth, Lindy Truswell, Liza Green, Lois Fort, Marguerite Poland, Marlese Naude, Matt Cullinan, Mervyn Sloman, Michelle Cooper, Mike and Coral le Sueur, Murray Rushmere, Ockert van der Schijff, Peter Siddons, Phillip Ihenacho, Pippa Hetherington, Rolf Lamprecht, Roshane Teddar, Sally Kaka MaNyawuza, Sara Dane, Sarah Mamobu, Sarah Rushmere, Shirley-May Williamson, Siv Stundal de Vos, Sophia van der Schijff, Sue Andrew, Sue Garland, Susan van der Schijff, Sybil Chambers, Tom van der Schijff, Vicky Crankshaw, Victoria Mayer, Wangui Th'anga, Yvonne Blackwood-Murray, and Zodwa Madikane.

This book is dedicated to my parents Diana and Jeremy Stubbs.

ABOUT THE AUTHOR

Nicky Stubbs has a talent for cooking that is appreciated by her enthusiastic friends and family. After lunch they lose their good manners and fight over the chocolate mousse bowl; at tea time they drop in unexpectedly in the hope of a freshly baked lemon sponge, and at supper time they can count on being invited to linger as there is always enough food for everyone.

Nicky's passions are family, friends, food and books. In her long and interesting career, she has completed a Cordon Bleu cooking course, cooked in London and France, run restaurants, catered, given cooking classes and written for magazines. She is currently the Sales and Marketing Manager of NB Publishers.

This Is Just to Say
I have eaten
the plums
that were in
the icebox

and which
you were probably
saving
for breakfast

Forgive me
they were delicious
so sweet
and so cold

William Carlos Williams,
1883-1963